D1609196

Also by
Gail Wilson Kenna

The Face of the Avila

The Story of a Contrary, Contumacious Cat

Here to There and Back Again

Beyond the Wall

www.gailwilsonkenna.com

Crosshill Creek Publications, LLC
P. O. Box 216, Wicomico Church, VA 22579

A Soul-Making

KEATS

Collection

A Soul-Making
KEATS
Collection

Award-winning writing of
Gail Wilson Kenna

Gail Wilson Kenna

Crosshill Creek Publications

First Edition Copyright © 2021 Gail Wilson Kenna

All rights reserved. No part of this book may be reproduced in any form
or by any electronic or mechanical means, including information storage
and retrieval systems, without permission in writing from the publisher,
except by a reviewer, who may quote brief passages in a review.

Printed in the United States of America

Crosshill Creek Publications, LLC
P. O. Box 216, Wicomico Church, VA 22579

This book was designed and produced by
Hearth & Garden Productions
A. Cort Sinnes, Design

Kenna, Gail Wilson A *Soul-Making Keats Collection*

written by Gail Wilson Kenna

ISBN 978-1-73410602-4-6

Front cover: Portrait of John Keats by
Charles Armitage Brown, pencil, 1819

Dedicated to poet and Soul-Making Keats director,
Eileen Malone, and to the SMK judges, past and present

Table of Contents

Prologue

P oet John Keats wrote, "I am certain of nothing but the holiness of the heart's affections and the truth of the imagination." I would add to his words, "and life's mysterious coincidences." Were it not for happenstance, I would not have attended the famous conference for writers in Vermont, the Bread Loaf. Chance also meant meeting a woman named Marie outside the historic Inn that first afternoon. Marie, I learned, had been a journalist in London years before, and she loved *Keats House* in Hampstead, which I'd visited in 1978 on a tour of Britain.

At some point during the ten-day conference in August 2011, Marie told me about the Soul-Making Keats. For the past two years she'd won awards in this literary competition and gone to San Francisco for the annual ceremony. Then, a day before the Bread Loaf ended, Marie left suddenly. I was handed a note. Marie's daughter was terribly ill, and Marie asked that I contact her in Connecticut

As it turned out, and on a whim, I applied for the 2012 Bread Loaf Donald Axinn Fiction Scholarship. This involved revising my 2011 submission, based on what I'd learned in my seminar with writer, Luis Alberto Urrea. Besides the revision, I had to submit a new chapter from my novel-in-progress, *Of Love and Circumstance*. To my surprise I won the scholarship. And in August 2012, on my way to Vermont, I stopped in Connecticut to see Marie.

While in the U.K. in the late 70s, I'd bought two large pen & ink drawings of *Keats House* in Hampstead and later framed them. I thought Marie might like one for her office at Sacred Heart University where she taught literature and writing. During my short visit, Marie again mentioned the Soul-Making Keats, told me its yearly deadline was November 30th, which meant I had time to put together a submission or two. Only printed submissions were accepted, which meant being read on paper, not a screen. I liked that idea. And on the SMK website, I could learn about the judges and requirements for the ten adult categories. Only five dollars per entry, and multiple submissions allowed. I could see that Marie admired this literary competition, an outreach program of the National League of American Pen Women (NLAPW). *Why not give it a try?*

I studied the SMK website. In particular, the Intercultural Essay interested me. I'd lived in Germany, Malaysia, Venezuela, Colombia, and Peru. Experiences from other cultures swarmed in me, just waiting to be given form in words. That November of 2012, I submitted "Malay Days," along with an essay for Creative Nonfiction, "Sisyphus on Crosshills." In early January of 2013, I received e-mail from the Intercultural Essay judge, Tara Masih. I had won first place. Later I learned "Sisyphus" had won second in Creative Nonfiction.

Of what importance is this? The Soul-Making Keats kept me writing when I wanted to quit. In 2013 at Bread Loaf, I'd met the editor of the Graywolf Press. She had asked me to send my novel, *Of Love and Circumstance*. This I had done. Then I waited for almost a year, hopeful each day when I went to the mailbox. Finally, Graywolf's rejection came in e-mail. Give it up, I told myself. This is folly. Stick to teaching literature and writing.

Yet a year later, when November 2015 arrived, I sent three

submissions to San Francisco. Then in early January of 2016, I learned I'd won three awards. The following year I decided to submit to five categories. Again, I won something in all of them. In e-mail from Eileen Malone, the SMK director, I learned the Creative Nonfiction judge was leaving after a decade. Eileen asked if I would like to take her place.

What a privilege for the past four Decembers to wander in diverse, creative nonfiction, soul-making worlds. I give each submission in my category a slow and careful read, with many entries read a second and third time, until I have a group of finalists. That's when it gets difficult. Then, after results from all categories are posted on the SMK website, I send e-mail to the three winners and those with honorable mention, plus other writers whose submissions have spoken in some special way. For me, communicating with writers far and wide, in the United States and even foreign countries, has been an unexpected joy of being the Creative Nonfiction judge.

Next year will be the 30th for the Soul-Making Keats literary competition, with its evocative theme from John Keats. "Some say the world is a vale of tears, I say it is a place of soul making."

Gail Wilson Kenna

Fiction

Wedding Night

I had not seen a photo of David's ex-wife, but I'd overheard the occasional conversation between his daughters about their mother. Grace and Sylvia had been at the civil ceremony that morning and dashed out after the luncheon. A simple affair everyone called it.

Months earlier David had booked a Westminster suite at the Marriott on the Thames. And before we were to leave to dine at *La Chapelle,* a French restaurant with Michelin stars, David wanted to take another shower. I had needed a bit of chocolate, something to offset my exhaustion from the day. As David disappeared into the suite's enormous bathroom, I stepped out the door, not realizing until I'd shut it that he had the two keypads.

In the crowded lobby most of the sofas were taken, yet among the throng of people I could not help but notice her. She sat in a chair beside a large Ficus, dressed in a black skirt, black tunic, and black shoes that resembled slippers. Not odd attire for London, though it seemed strange apparel for a cloudless summer's day with an unusually ardent English sun. She looked so terribly self-confident, her long highlighted hair twisted up, and held by a comb that sparkled in the light.

Passing the Ficus a second time, holding a tiny bag of chocolates in my hand, I once again noted the woman's blasé confidence. I stopped, hoping she might look up. But she just sat there, elegant and austere, with one leg across the other, and one soft shoe dangling from her arched foot. *You know her,* a voice whispered. But what were the chances of David's ex-wife sitting in the lobby of the Marriott? Then a tinge of memory, of a conversation between Grace and Sylvia, about their mother being a docent at the new Tate Modern. The museum was not far from the Marriott. Might David's ex-wife be resting here after a long day of leading tours? *But surely not in those soft shoes.*

Upstairs I knocked and, while waiting, realized it would be silly to mention the woman in the lobby. David opened the door and stood there, bundled in a fluffy white robe that he had not bothered to tie. He asked where I had been, reached for me, and one of his hands brushed the tiny bag I held.

"Oh, you and your sweets!" he said, laughing. "I should have known where you were."

It was then a compulsion like chocolate overcame me.

"I know this seems improbable, David. But might I have seen your ex-wife in the lobby? An older version of Grace, you might say."

"Sheila? Downstairs already? Did I not tell you? She's mad about the chef at *La Chapelle* and joining us for dinner."

Ménage a trois, as the French say.

In the beginning was our end … is what I say.

Wedding Night
Flash Fiction, Honorable Mention, 2015
Judge: Mary Kennedy Eastham

El Amor No Correspondido

Jose waited each day in the late afternoon until the American girl appeared at the corner of the last stall, and while she kicked her boots against the wood post, he watched her. For one year he had seen caked mud fall to the ground, and from one night to the next in his cot in the army barracks, he thought about the girl, saw her touching the horse, rubbing her nose against its neck, repeating *Camarico* in her soft Spanish. Looking through the window beside his bed, the window without glass, he dreamed she might speak his name and draw it out, in the same way that his thoughts of her extended into the night.

Each day he hurried from stall to stall until he reached the stallion, and then like the sun the girl appeared with carrots for the horse. The minute she rounded the corner and paused to kick her boots against the post, Jose took out a cigarette so he might hold something while she sank her face in the stallion's mane. He had groomed this horse longer than any of the others, carefully lifting each hoof to scrape away the mud, so each hollow of each hoof would be clean for her to fill again.

On afternoons when she competed in jumping, he was there, and when the horse refused a jump and officials waved the girl from the ring, he watched her chin begin to quiver. More than good food or a soft bed or a leather jacket, he wanted in that moment to hold and comfort the American girl. Yet while removing the saddle from the horse's back, he only shrugged and said, "*La proxima vez.*" There would be another time. Yet on days when the girl's eyes shone from clean jumps and a good round, he dreamed of holding her in his arms. In such moments he only said, "*Si, bueno.*" And she, chin quivering or eyes shining, saw the stallion *Camarico*, golden in the sun.

At night in his narrow cot, he imagined being her trough of water. Then he laughed at himself. He was not like the foolish village girls who came to Caracas, worked as maids, watched *telenovelas*, and dreamed of rich men wanting to marry them. He would serve his time in the army, return to his home near Merida, and marry a girl in the village. And in the tradition of his grandfather and father, he would feed a family from earth beneath his feet.

Yet on long nights when he tired of the stars and the cool night air, he recalled the afternoon when the girl had stopped at the last stall, knocked her boots against the wood post, and dropped her riding whip. One of her hands had held a salt lick and carrots. In the other hand was a pink box, which she pressed against her body to keep it from falling to the ground. Although he tried not to dwell on this memory during nights without sleep, he could not stop thinking about the American girl—her beautiful white teeth, her green eyes, her long dark hair that she gathered beneath her riding hat each afternoon.

It had been in that moment of watching the girl and lighting his cigarette when he heard her say, "*Una torta de chocolate para ti.*"

He knew a puzzled look had crossed his face.

"*Te gusta chocolate?*" she asked, handing him the pink box before she turned to retrieve her whip.

He had stood with the box in his hands. She had made the cake, she told him, not bought it at a bakery. Again, she asked, "*Te gusta chocolate?*"

"*Claro,*" he said, feeling a lump in his throat that did not disappear until the girl had ridden away, having forgotten her whip as she often did, which allowed the stallion his stubborn moments in the ring.

That afternoon he took a knife from the girl's large trunk that stored her equipment, and he scraped away the remnants of the old salt lick. As he removed the caked salt, he thought about her question. *Did he like chocolate?* She would never know that cacao was the crop of his grandfather and his father. The American girl would not understand the bitterness of *cacao,* or that one *cascara* of *cacao* held two nuts inside its shell. She knew only chocolate that had been refined and sweetened.

Looking at the pink box on the girl's trunk, he wondered what to do. Rats would find the cake in the barracks. Had she meant for him to share the cake? Share it with soldiers who mounted horses at midnight? Soldiers who claimed the army did not pay them enough for whores? If they saw the pink box with the cake they would laugh, call it *la cosita,* and lick the frosting with protruding tongues. They teased him often about the American girl, said she had bewitched him. *Quieres meter palo en la gringa?* When he gave no answer to their crude question about violating the girl, he heard loud laughter. *No importa.* His grandfather and his father had taught him to uphold honor through silence.

That afternoon the American girl returned late from the riding ring. As he removed the saddle, he felt the horse quiver beneath his hands, heard the girl whisper, "*Camarico.*" Then holding out her riding hat, filled with the carrots, she placed it close to the stallion's head and, just as quickly, pulled the hat away. And bare and glistening in the sun, the stallion followed the girl wherever she moved, pressing his head into her body until the carrots from her hat were gone.

Wrapping the reins around the bridle, he watched the girl and the horse moving in a circle. Turning away from them, he again saw the pink box on the girl's trunk, a *baul* as long and large as the ones that held weapons in the armory.

Dulce y amargo a la vez, he thought, though bitterness was not his way. And when the girl left that afternoon, he quietly said, *"Gracias por la torta."*

At dusk while he fed and watered his long row of horses, he thought of hiding the box in one of the burlap sacks that held muck from the stables. Yet burying the girl's gift in that way was no better than inviting crude words from soldiers. He could leave the box in the girl's baul, but the cake could not be there when she came to ride the following day, and they unlocked the trunk to remove the ointments and the special feed that cost more than a year of his pay. He never dwelt on fellow soldiers who stole money instead of buying feed, and he gave little thought to the officers who believed the riches of life were for them. But in thinking about his superiors, he remembered a huge magnolia tree that stood at the far end of the lake by the officers' club.

It had been a month since the soldiers had gone to the lake and stripped to their shorts and spent the day piling algae at the water's edge. At the sight of themselves covered with strange green tendrils, some soldiers had laughed. Others cursed. It had been that day, while enduring the slime and strong smell of the algae, when he had seen the beckoning white flowers of a magnolia tree near the lake.

Now, remembering the tree, he knew where he would bury the cake, leaving it untouched within the pink box, entrusting to memory an image for his solace.

After the stables were dark and the soldiers had gone to eat, he found a bag that had held feed. He placed the pink box inside it, then took his shovel and left the stables. At night there would be no boats on the water or runners circling the path around it. While walking the mile to the lake, he thought about his return home in a year. He would not talk about his time in the capital except to say that God had spared him the care of a horse belonging to the daughter of a Venezuelan army officer. The secret of his love for the American girl would never be known by his family and friends in the village. From words the girl had spoken, he knew she would return home for university. He did not know when that would be, but he prayed it would not be before his time in the army ended. Never would he know her mind or her body, but he could bury her cake in moonlight beneath the white flowers of the magnolia tree. And like the silver moon above the silent lake, this moment would fill and refill the hollows of his heart.

When he returned to the barracks that evening, and as he removed his boots, caked earth from his soles fell to the floor beside the cot. Lifting a clump of the caked mud, feeling the moist earth in his hands, he gave thanks to God that he would see the American girl tomorrow when she stopped at the wood post to kick her boots. She would call out to him, as she did each afternoon, *"Hola, Jose Luis,"* and the stallion already whinnying from his stall would be there, waiting to claim her love.

El Amor No Correspondido
Short Story, 2nd Place, 2016
Judge: Mary Mackey

Of Love and Circumstance

August 12, 1998. For decades I have squeezed *pedestrian* prose into measured columns. Now I've no need or desire to do this, Jenny—not in the story I will write for you. Here in the Sierra Nevada mountains, beside the California creek of my childhood and youth, I am listening to the caws of blue jays, to their harsh and uncensored cries, envying their hunger as they swoop down to steal my toast. I note the word *pedestrian*, which I have written above. I'm thinking of the noun, not the adjective that describes my conditioned, journalistic prose.

Your mother, the walker, and it is almost three months since I happened on a ceremony in Arlington at the National Cemetery, and only then did I recall the news aired months earlier about the Vietnam War's *unknown soldier*. After decades of errors and a cover-up about his identity, his name was to be determined at last through DNA, so he could be put to rest.

I parked that recent May morning in a lot near the military entrance to Arlington cemetery, knowing I could leave my car there for the time I would be away in New York and Bogotá. The flowers I carried with me were for April and, after leaving them on her grave, I planned to head down to Arlington's civilian entrance and take the Metro from there to Union Station in downtown D.C.

Normally, the parking lot by the military entrance is crowded; and outside the Old Post Chapel where funerals are held, six horses and a caisson usually wait. Not that day. In the lot were press vans, numerous military vehicles, the black sedans of D.C. dignitaries. It further surprised me to see a soldier posted at the tiny military entrance. Never once had I been stopped there. The young soldier on guard reminded me of a sentinel I'd seen one day, executing the solemn and hourly march in front of the *Tomb of the Unknowns*, the only sound the loud click of his heels each time he reversed his direction. But this soldier in his black dress uniform stopped me and said the entrance was momentarily closed because of the special ceremony for the *unknown soldier*.

The young man's eyes reminded me of April's, the same startling blue clarity, his cheeks ruddy from the chill and fog of a spring morning. I set my bag down and shifted April's flowers from one hand to the other. The protective cellophane around the roses crinkled and, with the sound, the soldier's eyes moved from my face to the flowers. I could only think to say that my daughter's grave was in the cemetery. "She was an aviator," I said.

A pained expression came into his face. Then glancing away, he gave a discreet wave and allowed me to pass by. My feet had begun to ache, and I knew I should have worn old shoes, not new loafers. Despite the discomfort, I walked quickly, not slowing to identify VIPs assembling at the *Tomb*. Staring straight ahead, I strode as if on a mission, holding the flowers, the other hand with a large bag, a smaller one slung over my shoulder.

Before long I left the hill of old gravesites and continued downward. I walked through familiar acres of small white headstones, eventually reaching the area of the most recent burials. You will not have forgotten it. At April's grave I left the six yellow roses, each in its own tiny vial of water, roses that would survive until I replaced them. Grief had suspended so much that was habitual.

But not the habit of placing flowers beside the white headstone with April's name, rank and service, and the dates of her birth and death. After being at her grave and speaking to your sister for solace, my habit was to walk the cemetery's winding road to the Kennedy memorial. The eternal flame burning there was a reminder I always needed, so I would remember what the Kennedy family had endured—of how misfortune and tragedy never seemed to end for them. Rose Kennedy's death in 1995 at the age of 104 was one year after Gene's death at 70. Rose had outlived my father, your grandfather, by 34 years. Both were Irish, with Rose upheld through faith, Gene sustained through stoicism.

Ever since April's burial in Arlington, I have stood before that eternal flame and recalled the losses that Rose Kennedy endured: son Joseph shot down in the English Channel in 1944, daughter Kathleen dying four years later in a plane crash, both John and Robert assassinated in a span of five years, two of Robert Kennedy's sons gone, David dying of a cocaine overdose, and Michael from a skiing accident. In front of President Kennedy's grave, I've thought of Jackie, there beside her husband, and Arabelle and Patrick with them: one stillborn, the other surviving a few days, and only Caroline and John Junior alive. Yet who is to say if the surviving children will have long lives. Each visit to the Kennedy memorial has reminded me that life unfairly distributes death, as it has in our family.

Yet on May 14th I did not have time to visit the Kennedy memorial. I had a train to catch. As I hurried from April's grave to the civilian entrance, a brilliant sun broke through the fog, as was later reported in the press. The *unknown* was not a soldier. He was a pilot … like April and Gene, and your father Rob in Bogotá.

1.

The train left Union Station that noon, the place beside me empty, until Baltimore when a small boy sat down, his mother across the aisle. He ripped the plastic wrapper off a game called *Mad Monster*, inserted batteries, and electronic noises began. When the first game ended, the boy showed me his score, said his name was Tyler, and wanted to know my name. His smile showed missing front teeth.

"Mama! Look what I got!"

His mother frowned and asked what he'd been taught to say. He muttered "Excuse me, please," and began a second game, its electronic whistles announcing each monster's death. His mother continued talking to her seatmate until the boy shouted again, and she demanded, "Let me hear it!"

"Excuse me, Mama. I'm hungry."

She dug in her bag and handed him a ten-dollar bill. He dropped his game beside me, tore up the aisle, only to collide with an agent who led the boy back to his seat. "No running in the train, son." The boy kept his head down and tugged at his long, white T-shirt. The mother stood and thrust her son's chin upward with the back of her hand. "What the man wantin' to hear, Tyler."

"It's okay," the agent said softly, his eyes catching mine as he turned to leave.

The mother took the boy's arm and pulled him up the aisle. Feeling her exasperation, I thought of children tethered to parents and wanting to be free of them. Outside the window, piles of old tires and walls of graffiti flashed past. A strong wind whipped the thin branches of anemic-looking trees, and a phrase, as if chattered on the rails, echoed my thought … *child as kite*. I remembered when Rob had wanted you and April to share his passion for aerodynamics and bought two kites. April had shown keen interest and listened to Rob's instructions. Not you, Jenny. You raced away, your dark ponytail swishing behind you on the parade ground of the Air Force base, and somehow with a beginner's luck, your kite rose steadily into the sky. Then you laughed and let go, and the fire-breathing dragon caught a fierce updraft, flew away unfettered, and disappeared. "That's the last kite I buy you," Rob said, not scolding, just stating a fact. We remained at the parade ground for hours that March afternoon, so Rob's willing recruit could fly her colorful bird.

Now, staring at the little black box, Tyler's *Mad Monster*, I silently recited familiar lyrics: *Close your eyes/ Have no fear/ The monster's gone/He's on the run/And your daddy's here.* On the aisle, the mother and son's seats remained empty. I doubted the boy's mama listened to John Lennon songs. *Life is what happens/ while you're busy making other plans.* Reciting lyrics usually blocked thought, but not with this remembered song — one from an album bought when the Beatles separated, most of our 33rpm collection gone or stolen during one move or another. Yet the lyrics remained — of tunes Rob had sung to you and April, like *Beautiful, Beautiful Boy*, the song no parent sang to him.

Soon the boy returned, slurping a can of Fanta. Why you and April preferred that sweet orange drink to other sodas, I never understood. But you hadn't grown up in Southern California as I had, when morning meant a glass of freshly squeezed orange juice from Gene.

Tyler offered me a potato chip and, between bites of his hot dog, again asked my name. Leaning closer to his sweet, mischievous face with its dabs of catsup, I teased that my name hadn't changed since Baltimore.

"So where you goin', Andreaaa?" he asked, drawing my name

out like a string of chewed bubble gum.

I said I was going to Colombia to see my husband.

"Columbia!" he blurted. "That's in Maryland. You on the wrong train."

I drew a big O in the air. "Bogotá, Colombia. A country far away."

"Well, me and Mama goin' to Philly," he said, and turned his game on, twitching beside me, never still for a moment. His mother was occupied with her seatmate and couldn't have known the favor she had done by sitting across the aisle. In Baltimore I'd been pleased to see the boy, had worried that a woman might take the seat and try to engage me in small talk.

When the train pulled into Philadelphia, Tyler jumped up, clasped his toy in one hand and thrust the other at me. Taking his hand, I said he had that monster on the run, "you beautiful boy."

"Mama, you hear what the lady say?"

Lifting her bag, the mother gave a small nod in my direction. "I hear … but she not be livin' with you, boy.

On the way to New York, I tried to push away thoughts of how foolhardy it was to go to Bogotá without telling Rob. But I felt unwise, as if grief's hunger consumed more than the heart. Still, clarity of thought told me one thing: In the U.S. embassy, Rob's work with intelligence agencies provided the means to trace your travel after London. To locate you was my need, and I would not listen to Rob's repeated claim that his daughter Jenny left Richmond College of her own free will, was twenty-one, and could make her own choices now.

From Penn Station, I walked to the Starbucks where I was to meet my friend Kate. At a long counter by the front window, facing the Southgate Hotel across the street, I watched young women jaywalking, as if immune to danger. Their self-confident strides reminded me of Kate. She had been reading manuscripts for Random House when we first met in the eighties. One evening in a small Greek restaurant in Soho, Kate had complained that every fourth novel from the slush pile was about a young woman arriving in New York and recounting a dream. "Who escapes clichés?" I'd asked, not mentioning how often Kate detailed her dreams. Even in my sleep I was a terse stringer, able to recall only a few images and never the narrative, until a dream shortly before April's death. Early morning at the seashore, a strand of kelp in my hands, a woman in white telling me about the root that holds kelp to the ocean's bed: the dream like the actual morning a few days before my mother died. We were on vacation at Newport Beach, Gene fishing from shore. I'd been jumping in a pile of kelp, enjoying the sound of excreted saltwater, until I'd slipped and fell into the slimy bed. Mother had lifted me up and held me against her pregnant belly. We had stood together for a long time at the water's edge, the sea casting foam onto our bare feet, innocent of the fury to come — of a Catholic hospital refusing an operation on a pregnant woman.

In Starbuck's from behind me, I sensed movement and turned. An unshaven man in a dirty white shirt, a sleeping bag in his hands, stood pigeon-toed a few feet away. Earlier, near Union Station in D.C., I'd passed a girl, her items for sale on a ratty blanket, a mangy dog beside her. I'd given her a few dollars, and now I handed a five to the man near me. Seeing a *New York Times* on another counter, I went over and retrieved it.

Flipping the pages of the first section, I searched for an article on the morning's ceremony and located a recap of the CBS January 19th 1998 story. The airman presumed to be in the *Tomb of the Unknowns* was Lt. Michael J. Blassie, formally known as X-26, his body consisting of six bone fragments, which had been exhumed for DNA testing in the early hours today. I'd begun reading the article a second time when Kate tapped my shoulder, apologizing for being late because something unexpected had come up at work.

Kate and I had not seen each other for over a year, not since April's funeral. Her hair was cut shorter, the shade of blond lighter. Sliding off the stool, I said she looked wonderful and hugged her. She ruffled my hair and asked if I wanted to eat in or eat out. I said cheese, crackers, and wine were all I needed tonight. Outside on the street, traffic was rushing past, and it was hard to hear what Kate was telling me about her new apartment. "It's narrow like a train," she shouted. "The double bed barely fits. Maybe it's time for a single."

"What if you met the love of your life?"

"I haven't," she said, shifting my bag to her other arm and telling me the bed was mine. Reminding her how poorly I slept and how often I got up during the night, I said the sofa was my choice. We soon stopped in front of a brownstone and went inside. Kate had not exaggerated about the flat being narrow. But she'd decorated it with her flair for wild colors like orange and red. She opened the sliding door in the small living room and invited me to sit outside in the garden while she uncorked the wine.

Sinking into a lawn chair, I watched lights coming on in the apartments above. Kate reappeared in jeans and a sweater, two bottles in her hands. "I bought your favorite red from the Napa Valley, a Louis Martini cabernet!" She poured the wine and handed me a glass.

"You doin' okay?" she asked. I knew the question had to do with my neglected appearance. I ran my hand through unruly hair, so much longer than the last time Kate had seen it.

"Am I okay? I'd be better if I'd brought warmer clothing."

"I'll get a shawl and some cheese. Then I want to hear about everything."

"Everything," I laughed. "You mean Jenny?"

"Yes, and Hylda, too," she said, opening the sliding door.

Sitting there in the fading light, I tried to remember what I'd told Kate about Hylda in phone calls and e-mail. Which details had stayed with her about this Victorian-Edwardian woman whose eyes obsessed me? Yet in the coming year, Kate would be able to see the first ever John Singer Sargent/Wertheimer exhibit at the Jewish Museum in New York; and if my interview went well, I might be asked to write an article for the exhibition's catalogue.

Of Love and Circumstance
Novel Excerpt, 2nd Place, 2015
Judge: Joanna Catherine Scott

Arrange Whatever Pieces Come Your Way

My deceased father's old leather suitcase could not be rolled, but London Heathrow provided free carts and intelligible signs to the bus terminal. After a cheery hello, the bus driver said it was early to board but to go ahead and take a seat. I assumed the coach was empty until I saw a man five rows back, dressed as I was: navy blue blazer, white Oxford shirt, khaki slacks. My impulse was to sit alone and absorb the scenery on the way to Oxford, but this man could have been a fellow reporter in Metro at the Post.

We introduced ourselves and he pointed to the seat beside him.

I said, "We could be twins, Cary!"

"I had the same thought, Kate. Except for our ages."

How could I not smile at this light touch on the thorniest of subjects—race? I liked him even more when, like a reporter, he asked to know three facts about me.

"Single, a journalist in D.C., infatuated with Inspector Morse. Your turn."

"Married, a chemist in Philadelphia, also a Morse fan."

As the bus filled, then left the terminal, we chatted. Everything seemed to amuse this sanguine chemist. Did his family like *Inspector Morse*? The question brought his laughter. Once he had convinced his son to watch an episode about an opera star and her visit to Oxford.

"The Rupert Murdoch character is in love with the diva? That one?"

"Yes. Do you remember the diva's hair stylist? A gay black man. My son still rags me about the stereotype. My wife's a psychologist. She calls Morse a melancholic grump."

"You're British?"

"Ugandan."

Uganda, the country Winston Churchill called the Pearl of Africa. I had written an extensive paper at Emory U. on Britain's peaceful withdrawal in the early sixties and Obote's rule until Amin's 1971 power grab. Now a direct source sat beside me, but I hesitated to bring up Idi's reign of terror.

"When did you leave, if you don't mind me asking?"

"In 1970. I've not been back."

I wanted to know but did not ask if his family had left.

"Well, you haven't lost your accent," I said.

"Nor you, yours!" he teased.

"I ought to! I open my Georgian mouth and my IQ plummets, unlike our President from Arkansas."

"Good old Bill Clinton. My son resists a nickname and insists on being called William. He says a princely name and a British accent exempt him from most prejudice."

"That's ironic," I said, explaining that colleagues at the *Post* chided me for being an anglophile, and even worse, a Southerner from Savannah, carrying around Flannery O'Connor and William Faulkner, defending two favorite writers against claims of racism. Saying this got me talking about the psychoanalyst I would be interviewing after Oxford, whose new book, *On Fear and Abandonment*, detailed her therapy with children who left Commonwealth countries, only to experience exclusion in the U.K. "Too much back story," I said, "as to why I was assigned to do this for

31

the *Post's* editor. Mainly, he wants to ping the BBC and the *Guardian* for their segments on racial discrimination at the *Post*, with many African-American reporters assigned to *Metro*." Feeling uncomfortable about getting into this, I told Cary that I'd come to Oxford to forget ethnic rage and urban blight.

A large truck passed the bus just then. Its noisy backfire muffled Cary's reply.

"Did you say we'll await the anecdote?" I asked.

"Antidote," he said, laughing. "But anecdote applies. Strangers at the crossroads. Two admirers of Morse?"

"Ah, yes! Crossroads. Carfax. How many times have we seen Morse in his red Jag drive past that famous monument?"

The bus had reached the outskirts of Oxford and slowed down on a tree-lined avenue. Near a bus stop, a lanky fellow stood at the curb. On his purple tee shirt in bold black letters, ***Fuck You***.

"High Street," the driver called.

"It's my stop!" Cary said.

I stepped into the aisle to let him out.

"Good-bye," was all I could think to say. I had not asked his last name or the location of his conference.

Moving over to the window, I fiddled with it. But I'm bloody helpless with anything mechanical and could not get it to open. I hoped that waving my arms would draw his attention. But Cary's head was lowered while the driver pulled out bags. He finally looked up and saw me, knocked his head with his open palm, as if the same thought had occurred to him. I could only be glad that Cary was looking at me instead of behind him. The fellow in the purple shirt was flipping him off.

If you visit a place in books or in a television series like *Inspector Morse*, it is possible to imagine illusory settings. No wonder the *Metro* staff chided me about my 'vacation' course. And that first morning in Oxford, as red double-decker buses rattled past, loaded with Asian tourists in orange headsets, I recalled the acerbic *Post* newsroom laughter directed at me. Just one block of Cornmarket curdled my first taste of historic Oxford. Turning my back on roaring motorcyclists, staring at a window, I read: *Our mission is to create handmade food, avoiding obscure chemicals.* "Good-luck to mission impossible," I muttered, walking past Burger King, opposite Mega-market. A squadron of pigeons flew past, ahead of a slow-moving truck. With my eyes on the birds, I noticed a second-story window with an old advert — the RCA dog with his nose in a Victrola. I wanted mine in a newspaper. The London papers had sold out, but accepting anything as my daily fix, I hurried back to Worcester College with *The Oxford Times*.

Seated on a stone bench beside Worcester Lake, one news article seized my attention. A brilliant Oxford student had hanged herself. "Extremely talented but wracked with self-doubt," the reporter asserted, along with a warning from the parents of Sarah Napuk: "Do not send your child to Oxford." The painful mystery of suicide, I thought, taking a few deep breaths, trying to push away thoughts of my father. *Time to take a vacation from newspapers.* But this admonition to myself did not solve an immediate problem.

The Oxford don for my writing course was a snobbish academic with a head of wild bushy hair, a man not much older than mid-thirties. He had given the class a stern warning. "No idle bones!" The nine other students were aspiring fiction writers: I, the lone journalist. Without hiding disdain when he heard my profession, Dr. Giles asked why I had selected a course on setting. "Thinking of venturing in fiction, are you?" During our first class, he asked each student to name an admired short story writer or novelist. When my turn came, I said, "Flannery O'Connor."

"Might she be a relative of the esteemed Frank O'Connor?" Dr. Giles asked.

"No ... but Flannery made Yale Professor Harold Bloom's list of 100 geniuses. The Irishman didn't."

A few students laughed. Dr. Giles ignored my comment, though several times during our first class he asked me to repeat something I had said, as if my southern accent were unintelligible. Eventually, he gave us our first assignment, which was to spend the afternoon wandering around Oxford.

Now hours later, gazing at Worcester Lake, I recognized my earlier folly. I had embodied the whole of Oxford with a sacred light, and it had dimmed on Cornmarket Street where commerce reigned. The Bodleian, I thought. And for the second time that day, I wound my way through the streets of Oxford — this time to its illustrious library.

In the English Literature reading room, I studied tense faces, not one without thick glasses. Most heads were lowered over old books, with white-gloved hands touching them. Only the stomp of a young woman's sandals on the cork floor disturbed the reverent silence. I jotted some impressions and left the Bodleian, having decided to visit the public library by the Westgate Shopping Centre and to compare the two libraries for Dr. Giles.

In the crowded reading room, old men in wrinkled suits filled the tables. Not one bore a resemblance to Morse. I chose a spot between an elderly man in a dark suit, who moved his chair to accommodate me, and a tall, thin fellow with long greasy hair, wearing a half-buttoned black shirt. His ratty motorcycle helmet rested on a stack of Want Ads. I had taken a seat just as a young black man sat down at the far end of the table. That's when I heard a particularly nasty racial epithet from the fellow beside me. He stood, hoisted his baggy jeans, grabbed his helmet, and left. I put aside the writing assignment and dug in my bag for the glossy postcard I had bought earlier with the newspaper. *Hello Metro ... You will be delighted to know that Aristotle Lane reeks of urine! Kate*

But the following morning I awakened with renewed spirits and left my tiny room in Worcester College. On Cornmarket I watched city workers in chartreuse vests turn on mighty hoses and disappear in clouds of steam, purging scum from the streets. The ablution, however, was not to last. By Oxford's oldest surviving building, the famous Saxon tower, I imagined Morse's red Jaguar speeding past. Nearby, a man in a fringed dress and floppy hat was unpacking things from a bicycle. I'd barely glanced at his cross-dressing attire when he screamed, "Fascist. You f...ing fascist."

Me? A fascist?

Then I realized the shouts were directed at a silver-haired gentleman in a dark suit. Feeling as if a magnet for sleaze, I retreated into Oxford's historic passageways where I found a necessary reassurance of the city's charm: ancient stone facades, doorsteps with empty glass pints beside polite notes: "No milk tomorrow, thanks." Beneath the skyline of spires, students in pressed uniforms bicycled past, and elderly women polished brass plates beside their doors. With a camera slung over my shoulder, I wandered on to Fisher Lane and paused on Quaking Bridge, peering at half a loaf of bread floating in the canal. The gray morning, dark water, the red and blue wrapper that kept the bread afloat. I said, "What a haunting photo!"

"Fuckin' tourist!"

I turned and saw the young man from the library. His unbuttoned black shirt flapped in the breeze, exposing a tattoo. I quickly looked away, though not before my eye caught an image on his bare chest of something ominous and dark.

In class that morning, Dr. Giles did not comment when I read my piece on two libraries. But later, looking directly at me, he said cotton in a writer's ear usually originates in the brain. The other students were polite and glanced away. For the next writing assignment, our don placed a map of Oxford on his desk and asked each student, one at a time, to mark it with a stickpin. I was the last to get a stab at the map and, given my academic record, ended up with the worst possible setting for a narrative—the Oxford science zone.

That afternoon I wrote in tiny print on an extra-large postcard. Dear Metro … I sit on John Pinto's memorial bench by Worcester Lake to let you know about Dr. Giles. This don expresses his opinion of oral prose through squinting. His tightly squeezed eyelids signal a verbal assault on his literary sensitivities. Unless a student reads with his or her head lifted, it is impossible to know the degree of pain one's prose inflicts on this arrogant fellow's sensitive ears. Are you laughing your heads off that I am vacationing here? Kate

On Saturday morning nothing seized my attention in the science zone except an advert for a web site, *God Thinks*. This, I concluded, rivaled the one for handmade food without obscure chemicals. While shaking my head I heard, "What *does* God think?"

Behind me stood Cary in a blue shirt, khakis, and polished shoes. He looked too dignified for a trek through Port Meadow. But I invited him to join me for free lagers, compliments of my Metro colleagues, many of them closet Morse fans. I said they had given me a beer glass stuffed with money and made me promise to drink lagers at the Inspector's beloved Trout Inn.

As Cary and I walked toward Walton Street, he commented that Oxford was much smaller than he thought it would be, and he had felt certain we would run into each other. I asked about the first week of his conference and was listening when I spotted the elderly woman and her two miniature white poodles. It was the third time I had seen the trio in as many days. "She calls them William and Harry," I whispered. "Don't they remind you of old tee shirts in need of bleach?"

The dogs were encircling a lamppost in opposite directions, the woman trying to balance a large bag in one arm while holding leashes in the other. She looked up, saw us, and laughed. "Harry's a good dog but never gets it right." Pulling on one leash, she told William to stand still. Cary offered to hold the bag of groceries, which freed her hands to untangle the poodles. She got them separated and, wishing us a good day, jaunted off with her courtly dogs.

"I admire anyone that sprightly and cheerful, especially in old age. Not someone caustic like the don for my writing course. Dr. Giles claims the Greeks took blood and excrement and made poetry, that most journalists replicate *merde*. At least he used the French."

Cary gave a coy smile and chuckled. "I suspect the don finds you attractive. And if we are to believe Morse, Oxford dons reek of envy."

"True of chemists?"

"Are chemists not human?"

Sneaking glances at his handsome face, I sensed Cary was a man without the infectious cynicism of most journalists I knew.

We reached a small red bridge and crossed it. After days of feeling cloistered, I loved Port Meadow's open sky and vast fields. Feeling light-hearted, I kidded Cary about his nice shoes as we wove our way through cow patties, some fresh, others white and crumbling. To avoid the new piles, we kept our eyes to the ground while we talked. I heard about the paper he would present on Monday and how he had spent his free time: visiting famous sites and drinking pints with other chemists at a Morse haunt, The White Horse.

"Speaking of Morse," I said, pointing to the river. "He could tell us ... Isis or Cherwell?"

"Isis," Cary said.

A flotilla of ducks swam past, two swans at the rear. When the white swan came to the riverbank, its gray mate remained in the water. In silence, not moving in the slightest, Cary and I observed the white swan. I wondered if Cary's work as a chemist had instilled this patience in him. I would not have given Dr. Giles the pleasure of agreeing with him. Yet I did share his disdain of hackneyed language, deadlines that promote clichés, and journalistic haste to get *the* story. I thought about the article I needed to write after Oxford, and the psychoanalyst's book on racial prejudice. Dr. Graves argued that Britain had turned migratory beings into strangers in a country they hoped would welcome and shelter them. Had Cary, with his British accent, been treated more fairly in the United States than he would have been in the U.K? Glancing sideways, seeing his amber eyes and unlined face, I wondered about his exile from Uganda and his family there. I thought of Father's suicide and felt familiar compression and pain in my chest. I turned quickly and my sudden movement startled the swan. Hissing, it raised its enormous wings and, in a blur of white, left the bank and rejoined its mate in the river. Then resting necks on folded wings like feathered fortresses, they floated away.

"What a marvelous creature," Cary said. "I've read swans have upwards of 75,000 feathers."

Cary turned his head toward me as he spoke. "Is something wrong, Kate?"

The question that came to me was an evasion of his.

I had to know if his parents had stayed in Uganda.

Under Port Meadow's darkening sky, Cary told me that his father had been the best-trained medical doctor in Uganda. President Obote's personal physician. A post unrelated to politics. Yet this position had made him an enemy of Obote's henchman, Idi Amin.

I asked how Cary had ended up in the United States, a year before Amin began executing Obote's supporters.

His father, he said, had anticipated the danger and sent Cary to a boarding school in Pennsylvania. Shortly after the coup, his father's disemboweled body was found. No one ever saw his mother again. Granted political asylum in Pennsylvania, he later became a U.S. citizen.

I swallowed hard several times before I asked how he could stand knowing that Amin was living safely in Saudi Arabia.

"My parents were two of the three hundred thousand who died. Some say a more accurate number would be a million. Either number keeps the personal in perspective."

By then we had reached the Godstow Locks, where we sat on a cement ledge near the river. I did not know what to say, and gratefully listened while Cary explained the simple and ingenious process by which a boat passes through locks. While sitting there, waiting for a boat to arrive, I told Cary about *my* physician father, who could have medicated himself for depression or sought help. Instead, after medical personnel left the Savannah clinic one late winter afternoon, Father placed one black towel on his desk, another on the seat of his chair, and shot himself. His nurse later explained the towels. Your father, she said, always the gentleman. He wanted to spare her a bloody mess in the morning. In a letter to Mother and me, he asked our forgiveness, said he was *a relic of old doctoring* and could not practice medicine as it was being prescribed to him now.

I stopped talking and reminded Cary of my profession; that as a journalist I relied on telling, not showing; that until I came to Oxford and heard Dr. Giles talk about the Greeks, I hadn't truthfully asked myself why I choose the profession.

"Now I know. Because I can't make poetry out of the blood of your father and mine."

Cary listened with one index finger across his mouth, a thumb under his chin, not speaking, only occasionally nodding his head. I found his gesture reassuring. Then, until a canal boat arrived and passed through the Godstow Locks, we sat in silence. When we could no longer see the boat, Cary reached down, pulled up a long piece of grass, placed it between his lips, and made a whistling sound from what he called, *our innocent past lives.*

"I knew we had more in common than a mutual appreciation

of Morse," he said. "Shall we call it the waters of affliction and fix our eyes on the road?"

By then the sky seriously threatened rain. We walked past the ruins of an ancient nunnery, saw a bridge and below it a gate, which my guidebook cited as a landmark to the Trout Inn. Beside the bank of the Isis, I spotted a young man holding a long fishing pole. He was seated between two adolescent girls. Poised on the bridge, a second young man waited, as if preparing to execute a backward dive. He was waving over his shoulder to the three on the bank, a short distance from the path we were on.

"That's an amazing fishing pole," Cary said.

The man on the bank tossed a beer bottle over his shoulder. Then he looked to see who had spoken. That's when he yelled to his mate. The young man on the bridge turned in our direction, his bare chest exposing the dark tattoo I had glimpsed on Quaking Bridge. I grabbed Cary's arm, hoping to hurry him toward the gate that would put us beyond the river. We had taken only a few steps when the taunt came, as I knew it would.

"Piss off nig."

It is now over twenty years since that rainy day on the Trout's terrace. A new series on Masterpiece Theater, *Endeavour,* led me to my files for this unfinished story. From the time of Inspector Morse's death on November 15th in 2000, I have missed him. Then in 2012, a Brit named Russell Lewis created the young Morse, whom I find enchanting: his sweet, pensive face, his squeamishness around corpses, his ardent love of opera and crossword puzzles, his yearning for a father figure, which he finds in Detective Inspector Fred Thursday of the Oxford police.

In the folder with the story was my certificate from Dr. Giles. He had placed a page limit on our final submission. I'd wiggled on the font and spacing to cram my story into twelve pages, the experience raw and unprocessed then. My ending was the young racist hollering to the wise Ugandan émigré, "Piss off, nig." No surprise. Yet I hoped situational irony might give meaning.

The last day of class, Dr. Giles announced that our narratives would be read aloud. Knowing how I had mocked him, I considered slipping out the door. But for my IRS tax credit, I needed the certificate. During our final class, Dr. Giles transcended squeezed eyes with most students, though not with me. Several classmates held hand to mouth when I read my story with its numerous digs at the don. Giles did not comment on our work in class but scheduled a fifteen-minute tutorial that afternoon with each student.

Hours later, re-entering our classroom off the Worcester quad, I expected and received an icy reception. Dr. Giles said I had fulfilled the requirement of a detailed setting, though he thought Oxford had been made overly sleazy. Furrowing his brow, as he often had in class, he asked what my story was about, not pausing to hear an explanation. "If education is the idea," he said, "the meaning eludes me, as abstractions always do in fiction. Is your story about repeated appearances?" he asked, running a hand through his bushy hair. "You give this great weight. A stab at the esoteric, perhaps? Or am I to conclude your real intent was to reveal this American woman's romantic glaze, hole and all?"

His questions were rhetorical, and I said nothing. Dr. Giles did ask to know the ratio of fact to fiction in the story before he assigned my grade, which along with my certificate would be at the Porter's Lodge when I left the college.

Hoping to leave without any further misunderstandings, I recalled the don's quip the first day of class. He had sniped that all he knew about Savannah was the overrated film, *Midnight in the Garden of Good and Evil*. The memory of this comment told me to enunciate my every word for his refined ear.

"I am a journalist," I said emphasizing the three syllables of my profession. "My story is only factual ... not fiction."

I had hoped to see a tiny shudder, the smallest of recognitions that the afflictions were real; and that in grasping this, Dr. Giles might pass through the locks of his prejudice; and in a rise upon the waters, that he might forgive my irreverence to him. This did not happen. And discounting science courses, I received from Dr. Giles the most mediocre grade of my life.

Now memory returns me to the ivy-covered Trout Inn where countless peacocks screamed from eaves, and sensible patrons moved inside to escape the rain, which ran steadily off the umbrella above the table on the terrace where Cary and I sat that afternoon. Had I been with my Metro colleagues, whose money paid for our lagers, I would have felt the fool sitting there, wordless and crying. Yet the Ugandan émigré knew there can be distilled meaning in silence.

Eventually I spoke, as I had to know how a bigot's slur simply washed off like rain. Simple, as Cary saw it. He regarded the young man in the same way that he thought of persons with an

43

allergy to brown rice or to white flour. *Hypersensitivity to a foreign substance.*

Other than these memorable words, I can only paraphrase what Cary told me that afternoon at the Trout Inn. He said we must keep trying to find the antidote to counteract the poison; and until that happens, we must live with acute awareness of the human history of hatred and massacres. Yet despite consciously knowing this, we must through actions embody a fervent belief in a fairer and more upright world. Then, reaching in the pocket of his khakis, Cary withdrew a postcard. He had bought it at Blackwell's bookstore on Broad Street without understanding why. "Now, I know," he said, handing me the card.

I hold it now. The card has the look of William Morris wallpaper. And in bold black letters are the words: **Arrange Whatever Pieces Come Your Way.** I kept this card in a box, along with the letters that Cary sent each New Year's from 1998 until 2007, when I did not hear from him. In February of 2008, his wife Tamara wrote to me about Cary's sudden death in late December from a heart attack. She asked if I would like my letters returned, which Cary had kept since the summer of 1997. I did ask for the letters—to remind myself of mysterious crossroads and bridges to persons and events that bring change, which is what Oxford had been. It was there I realized that if I wanted to be more than a *Metro* hack, I would have to struggle to become an investigative journalist who dug with courage and conviction for factual truth. But as young Endeavour Morse learned, there must be something to take away the darkness of policing the real world. For Morse this was music and literature. For Cary it was his family and chemistry. For Father it had been medicine as he believed it should be practiced. And what is it for me, a reporter, who investigates corruption, hatred, and violence? I have found my antidote in writing fiction — arranging thoughts and images in whatever mysterious way they come.

The Greek dramatist Aeschylus, who made poetry out of blood, claimed that *even in our sleep, pain that cannot forget* the poisonous day, *falls drop by drop upon the heart.* I keep this quote on my desk, read it each day, to help keep infectious cynicism at bay. These words from Aeschylus are an antidotal yeast, like my borrowed mantra from Flannery O'Connor.

Everything that rises must converge.

Arrange Whatever Pieces Come Your Way
2020 NLAPW Biennial/Letters
Central New York Branch
Flannery O'Connor Short Story Award, 2nd Place

As Deadly as Ever

June 1985. This morning I walked into Mr. Stein's office with my note pad to record the latest changes to the upcoming winter catalogue. Usually when I walk in, he has his big chair turned to the window and is looking down on Market Street in smoggy downtown L.A.

But today he stood and said, "Congratulations, Chandra."

If this surprised me, what had surprised him was going to the L.A. Art Museum with his son Jacob, home from Yale for the summer, and seeing the new exhibition of my work. Mr. Stein said he had known about my earlier show but had no knowledge of this one. His son's minor, he told me, is Fine Arts, and Jacob would like to meet me. Could I join them on Sunday for Jacob's twenty-first birthday celebration?

I thanked Mr. Stein and said it would be my pleasure.

He opened the mock-up for the new catalogue, then held the cover between his fingers, and asked a question that surprised me. He wanted to know what had led to my success in photography.

I already knew I had little time to answer Mr. Stein. And I paused, so he would take in my name, and told him that in Sanskrit, Chandra means … she outshines the stars. Then I added that a few proud moments in life had made all the difference.

"Proud moments," he repeated, "Couldn't agree more."

Was he thinking that I meant trophies and A's? Not at all what I was thinking. But I was not about to explain myself to a man who does not want a minute of his time wasted.

Later, when I left the office and got in the elevator on the top floor, I thought about myself, eighteen years earlier, riding the big yellow bus to Price Junior High. Would time discount the importance of those years? Make everything fade like old photographs that nobody thinks to preserve? By the time the elevator stopped on the second floor, I had decided to put my memories on paper. But just the way the words came to me, not tongue-tied by the language from school. I would write the voice I heard from way inside, the voice of Dee Dee, as I was known back then, in 1967.

1.

I don't know what I see first in my mind — the big yellow bus or skinny ass me. I never did slump down to not look so tall. Everybody always saying ... girl, you all bones, acting like I got a disease or something. I all legs and long arms, and I got the biggest 'do' on my head, all frizzed out, not all neat bothered like my ma Riva's hair. I all wild looking and it be that girl I see on the big yellow bus.

I never forget rising early, waiting with the bus kids, then riding through San Pedro. First we choke in smog. Then me and that bus of black and brown faces rise to the peaks above the ocean — to that all nice white school where the bus it stop and we get belched out. We suppose to scatter. But we all clump like burned bits in the cream of wheat. For three years I sit in class with the same kids from the bus, then ride home and play with the same kids in the streets. And this my Uncle Nat say, what they call integration.

But the bus kids get revenge. We make it real tough for teachers who get us. Below average. That's what they call the classes the bus kids in. Most of the teachers not willing to fight us, mostly shut us up, tell us to copy out of books, stuff like that. I carry a big bag to school, all full of magazines and books that Nat give me to read. My uncle help me a lot, kind of thinking it his responsibility since my white daddy in the navy never come around much.

The first day I go to Price, I tell Nat about the mess I get in with the Dean of Girls. Miss B we call her. From day one she after me cause the summer before junior high I grow about six inches and my skirts crawl way up my legs. But I look in magazines at the beauty shop where Aunt Lavinia work, and I see real tall ladies wearing dresses that barely cover their ass and that's what they call fashion. I think I be fine in my short skirts. Miss B not agree. She got corkscrew curls all over her head like some old blue-hair lady wear, only Miss B's hair blond. And I know it dyed cause the roots be showing. What's worse is Miss B's stockings with big ugly seams. That something I never see. Miss B wear real ugly suits too, all brown and gray, covering that big chest. She got the biggest lungs you ever see — like a thrush bird about to bust out in song. Only no song come from her.

I never forget what Miss B ask me the first day at Price. "Do you enjoy being indecent?" That's what she say. Then Miss B read me the dress rules. The way she tell it I got nothing to wear.

So that night I tell Nat what happen at Price and how Miss B waiting outside the bus with her yard stick. He ask how Miss B look, sniffing round the girls' legs, measuring hems. Without thinking I say, "She look indecent."

"That's my point, Dee Dee. It sound like Miss B got her own kind of problem. So this what you gotta do. You look her in the face and say, this all I got to wear. She know not to mess with you."

I tell Nat I got no interest in looking in Miss B's face cause her eyes pinpoint and piercing.

"You let her know, Dee Dee, that you not the kinda girl to

bug."

My uncle Nat know more than anybody. So I do what he say. Day two at Price I don't sneak away like the other bus girls do. I stand real straight and look in Miss B's face. Matter of fact I so tall I looking down.

"Miss Braithwine," I say real slow like. "This all I got to wear." She look at me like I not even there. But Nat be right. Miss B don't bug me. But she watching me just the same.

⟡

I go to Price Junior High grade seven, eight, and part of nine. Then after years of copying out of books and doing a crossword puzzle like it some prize in the caramel corn box, Miss Sims come along to second period below average English class.

She got blond hair piled on her head and pale skin like the Ivory soap ads and she wear a black dress that look like a coat, same as I see in the fashion magazines. She got pink in her cheeks and blue eyes and her hair it all fine and straight. I sit there, wondering where her hair fall if she let it down. The boys all jabbing each other and doing little chicks and clucks.

Then the principal walk in and the class get real quiet. Mr. Meadows talk about Miss Sims, how she a 1967 graduate, just beginning her career, and he know we gonna make her feel welcome. Mr. Meadows be old, about to retire he say, and his eyes both sad and blue. He never quite straight when he walk like the ground be hurting him.

When Mr. Meadows leave, Miss Sims start passing out a paper. "If you could make three changes in your life, what would they be?"

My answer come quick to her dumb question.

First, I be pure black.

Second, I be very rich.

Third, I hire a lily white maid in a black dress.

Miss Sims she walking round the room and I feel dislike positively creeping over my skin. Then she stop in the far corner and I see her in full. She got ugly legs. Her body not fat. Round I suppose you say. But her legs real big like she done sports or dancing. Girl in gym class got legs like that and she tell me ballet give her big calves. Well, Miss Sims got 'em too, and in my mind they make a mess of her looks. So I say out of the corner of my mouth, "She not bad lookin' but she got legs like an elephant."

My words bust up the bus kids and get the hoots and slaps going.

"Quiet, please," Miss Sims say, looking from face to face till she stop on mine. I think there no way she know that I the culprit cause she way by the other side of the room when I open my mouth. But her eyes stuck on me. Then she shrug and smile at the same time, and she tell us it better to be an elephant than a cross between a tarantula and a black widow spider.

Oh, and don't the bus kids love it, thinking it cool the new teacher know the game bottoms and she put me down, not ignore my smart mouth words. But I sit all wrapped round my desk, feeling almost embarrassed by my long legs and long arms and wishing I had a place to stick all of me out of sight. Then something come quick and I say, "Hey, teacher lady. You gonna get in a mess of trouble for that race slur."

"I wasn't referring to race," she say, laughing like everybody except me. Then she begin reciting a poem about dreams and what happen if dreams get deferred or you got none. I think she putting us on, but I don't reach in my big bag for something else to do that day.

50

The bus kids give Miss Sims a bad time. But she don't give up like some teachers do. She keep trying new things and when something don't work, she try again. She make Friday a special day and say we can have free reading. That's funny cause most of the bus kids can't or won't read. And that first week nobody remember their book and after the spelling test that every kid at Price take on Fridays, we got nothing much to do. Miss Sims sit on her desk and ask questions about us. Soon the room be mostly quiet.

That's when I see Mr. Dicks prowling round outside the open door. Miss Sims flash us a funny look and slide off her desk and kind of blow over to the door and shut it.

"Hey, Miss Sims," Tony say. "You better watch out for Mr. Dicks." The class crack up cause Mr. Dicks such a sparrow wing of a dean when you compare him to Miss B. But I can see Miss Sims got no idea why we laughing.

When Monday come and the bus kids roll into class, Miss Sims ask if she can trust us.

I hear this and slap the side of my head the way Nat do when something too dumb to believe. Don't Miss Sims know she looking at a cast of crooks? Joe and Raphael in the marijuana business, and when they ask to go piss, they moving stuff round the lockers. And Willy Crutcher? He pick your eyeballs if he think they locks. But Miss Sims sitting on her desk, hair all pulled back with a gold scarf, asking about trust.

51

Nobody answer her question, so she go on talking. I ramsack my big bag cause I can't think what she got to say gonna be all that interesting. Then she start telling how Mr. Dicks stop her on Friday and say that she commit a big sin of the teaching profession. He tell her that sitting on her desk lose her the respect of her students. Miss Sims ask us to write down what we think about that.

I write that I don't mind if the elephant sit on her desk, long as she keep her trunk out of my business. I 'bout to sign my name just like John Hancock when I think to say … "Mr. Dicks bound to Miss B. That's why Tony say to watch out for him."

The next day we get our papers back and I see what Miss Sims write on mine.

I grab a big fat dictionary and look up the word, real relieved ASTUTE mean better than it sound.

2.

One day in March Miss Sims tell us to meet in the auditorium the next day for the annual talent show. She think the show be a big treat. When we meet in the auditorium on Friday, we got rotten seats in the middle section but way at the side. Miss Sims, she not think to assign us seats like the other teachers do, so the rowdy dudes all together and Miss Sims at the end of the row. The bus boys no sooner slump down than their feet go up. The theater in our part of Pedro full of old men jerking off or low types who do it on the floor. I put my feet up there too, so I don't get sticky stuff on my soles. But in the auditorium at Price, Miss Sims want us to sit up like we royal — feet flat, backs straight. That don't last long 'cause the first act make the bus kids scream with laughter. Aletha and me almost pee our pants. Bunch of skinny white girls with no hips and no tits trying to dance to the Temptations.

Tony yell, "Give it to me, baby."

Then the big green velvet curtain draw shut.

When it open, I see a girl on a bar stool—only the stool come from a teacher's room, not no bar. The girl got rolls round her middle and she wear a sweater that make her look like she got no neck. She Anna somebody, a nice Italian girl from gym class, singing like that Barbara somebody with the big nose. Only Anna got no talent and she way off key. I embarrassed for her and wish Anna would stop singing 'bout people needing people being the luckiest people in the world.

"You weren't lucky, baby!" Tony holler.

Just then I get an elbow in my ribs. I 'bout to smack Rafael for hitting me when I see the bus kids looking at Miss Sims. The curtain closing on Anna but we got our eyes on Miss B who standing there. She got her arms 'cross that big chest and she look mad. Miss Sims leave her seat and go to the back of the auditorium. Miss B stand beside us. We don't make no noise for the next eighteen acts.

On Monday we forget what happen and shove our way into class like always, only Miss Sims not talking and she already got our work on the board. Pretty soon there be nudges and whispers round the room.

Willy Crutcher say real loud, "What got her?"

"Oh, she just playin' kick the dog," I say.

"What's that?" Gary Green ask.

"Oh, you know, lame brain. Somebody get in trouble and get

all mad, so they kick the dog."

"Why do that?"

"Cause he ain't gonna kick back, idiot."

We keep jiving until I see Miss Sims walking my way. She ask what I wanna say. So I think, tit for tat, lady.

"What you wanna say be more like it?"

"You stayed real quiet when Miss Braithwine was there," Miss Sims say, taking a gulp like she need air for another burst. "I guess you like to be treated mean, told to shut up, stomped into the ground."

I turn my face to the back wall. That's what I do when somebody miss the mark. The bus kids got their mouths shut, all guilty like. But I mostly mad.

"You got it all wrong, teacher."

She answer real smart like. "Do set me straight, Dee Dee."

"How many wanna be there Friday?"

Nobody raise a hand.

"See Miss Sims. You think we wanna be there."

"Maybe you didn't want to be there. But that's no reason to be rude. How would you feel … being laughed at on a stage?"

"That's my point, Miss Sims. You ever hear Carlos sing? You ever see Aletha dance?"

She look right smug when she answer. "If some of you have talent, why weren't you in the show?"

"That's my point, Miss Sims. How we gonna be in the show? You gotta stay after school for practice. But there's no late bus 'cept for boys' sports, and that bus all filled up."

Miss Sims start walking round the room. She look a little mad, too. She say if she ran the talent show, she'd have the practices at noon. "We'll write a letter to let the administration know it's not fair to exclude bus kids. You can take our letter to Mr. Meadows,

Dee Dee." Miss Sims smile at me, right proud of her words.

"That all be very nice. But that's our last Price talent show."

"Yes, I know it is. But sometimes we do things for those who follow."

The room get real quiet till Miss Sims let out a little cry and say, "I know what we'll do! We'll have our own talent show in the little theater."

That week and part of the next we get ready for our show. Richard and me and five others write a play called *Hold up in a Grits Factory*. Every kid in class busy with something, even Gary Green, our token white boy. Rafael, the Mexican muscle man, fancy himself the boss of somebody like a boxer or rock star, and he convince Miss Sims to appoint him the organizer. He keep getting excused from class to check out the theater. We all know he doing his dope deals, but Miss Sims look on him with trust.

All during the days we work on the show, I hear that Tony organizing his band and they gonna bring electric gear to school. The Wednesday morning of the show, Miss Sims plan to meet Tony so he can set up. But our bus break down and we get to school late.

Second period, we meet in the theater. The Hominy Grits play gonna be first, but Miss Sims give Tony time to set up his band. Everybody spread out in the theater to practice whatever they gonna do. I the poor innocent victim of the robbery and I busy getting robbed. I remember Aletha dancing to a Smokey Robinson song 'cause I hear it. And I remember Rafael working the lights and Raul and John tuning their guitars and Tony playing his drums. Then Joe come from behind the curtain and everybody plug in their speakers and Tony get his band going on a tune. The music so loud we kinda blasted away. That's when Miss Sims walk down the aisle to get Tony's attention. I can see that Raphael know what Miss Sims want but he enjoy his power more. Miss Sims walk to below the stage. Tony don't look at her cause he looking at what we all see in the doorway.

Miss B shout, "Unplug the speakers. Who authorized use of this theater?" She say this real loud and mean.

Everybody turn from Miss B in the back to Miss Sims in the front.

"I reserved the theater for our talent show."

"Is this an English class?"

"Well, yes, but ..."

Miss B say the Little Theater not meant for English class talent shows with electric guitars, and she want everybody back in the classroom and the theater left as we found it.

"Is that clear, Miss Sims?"

It clear that what Miss B want.

What I want is for Miss Sims to grab the curtain and swoop into that old bat's head and knock her back in the dark where she belong. But what Miss Sims do is plead that the class go to a lot of work to plan the show.

Miss B cut her off. "I have a meeting next door and you have a class to teach in your room." Then she stomp out.

Nobody say much. It get real quiet, the kind of quiet that come with disappointment, like when you hope for something at Christmas and don't get it. When this happen, I don't like to hurt nobody's feelings so I keep my mouth shut. Nothing new 'bout disappointment for the bus kids, so maybe we not take it as hard as Miss Sims. We collect the programs, scoop up the grit boxes, unplug the guitars and record player, and haul everything back to class.

I feel sad for Miss Sims. But she make me mad, too.

In the classroom, Aletha say, "Hey, Miss Sims. Why you not be a dean? You be a nice one. Not no bag like Miss B."

Miss Sims don't say nothing. But later I tell Aletha that to be girl's dean you got to be old and mean and wear stockings with seams.

The talent show a flop. But Miss Sims don't give up on the letter. She get us to write it, and every bus kid sign it, and I take the letter to Mr. Meadows. I like him so I not mind one bit. He ask me inside his office and, sitting there, I begin to tell what happen in the little theater. In his eyes I see that he not like what he hear 'bout the show that never happen. But in his eyes, along with what sad and blue, I see little sparkles like he laughing inside. Maybe that's 'cause I so good at telling a story.

The next week, Miss Sims read us a letter from Mr. Meadows. He write that he not be at Price next year. But he promise the bus kids get a chance to be in the talent show. And everybody cheer, cause it's what you do for a victory, even if it be small.

During the first week of May, Miss Sims real excited, like the good thing she been waiting for come true. In her hand she got a second letter from Mr. Meadows and she look right proud. She fix her eyes on me and tell the class that Mr. Meadows would like Dee Dee to be a model in the annual fashion show. The bus kids all looking at me, and for once I got a bare cupboard of words. I think how I sit for two years and watch the grade nine models strut by. I know I tall and thin enough to model clothes from Buffum's, that fancy store in Long Beach. But the girls they always white and don't ride no bus to school, and a girl tell me you got to wear your own shoes for the show. How I gonna manage that? But I got to say something. Only one thing come to mind that gonna make the bus kids laugh.

"Miss B, she be real happy to have me."

3.

The month of May feel like somebody spill 7 up on it. I see clear but things sticky to touch. From the first fashion show meeting it obvious that my being a model no plum in Miss B's bowl. She look at me like I big and rotten and full of fruit flies. But the department store lady from Buffum's tell me that I tall and thin enough to be a real model. She don't bring junior dresses for me. No! She bring fancy stuff from what she call the designer boutique. The last outfit she show me, I like the best. She lift a black hat from a box. The hat got a big white ribbon 'round the brim. I thinking that black on black not my choice, but she unzip a bag and take out a white suit and tell me to be careful 'cause the material wrinkle. She mostly curious about my feet since we got to wear our own shoes, so she write down what I need to wear with the suit. Where I get the money to buy a pair of fancy, black patent heels? But I know Nat help me out if Riva too broke.

I try not to act like the fashion show a big deal. The boys get a baseball game so they not be there to hoot and holler. A big stage get built outside and stay there till the graduation assembly. The department store lady, Miss Carson, arrange for me to be the last model—that after every outfit worn, she want me to come out in the white suit and black hat.

But the day of the show I do something real dumb. The blouse and pants I wear look good with my flat shoes. And the fancy formal so long and full that Miss Carson tell me to wear my flats 'cause they won't show. But I got to have the black heels for the white suit. Riva buy the shoes and make me walk 'round the living room every night for a week, telling me I got to stride and not clunk.

The morning of the show I so excited that I forget the shoe box and not think a thing 'bout it till I get a note in Miss Sims' class and go to the office like the note say to do. The secretary call my house and hand me the phone, and it then I hear Riva yelling 'bout the shoes and how she spend grocery money to buy 'em and how I do such an idiot thing.

I tell Riva not to worry, that I be home at lunch to get my shoes. But Riva right 'bout one thing. Home not next door. Just then Mr. Meadows happen by, real friendly like, and I tell him my problem. He give me a note for Miss Sims and say she can drive me home during lunch. After I leave the office, I sneak a look at the note and see that Mr. Meadows tell Miss Sims not to worry if we get back to school late, that he cover her class.

Gym class right before lunch, and what with the fashion show in the afternoon, I take a long time in the shower and get to the parking lot late to meet Miss Sims. She there, sitting in her little blue car. It not much bigger than me and I can't see where to put my legs. But she push at something under the seat and it slide back.

"What you call this?"

A VW bug."

"It a bug all right."

She tell me we got to hurry. But her bug it putt along. Even with the seat back, my legs all the way to the dash. Then I think that Miss Sims and me got time in that little car, that I never talk to her alone.

When we stop for a light at the bottom of the hill, she look over and smile. "You've been different around me lately. Not teasing so much. Why is that?"

I sit there not knowing what to say. Lucky for me, she go on talking.

"I feel you're disappointed in me?"

I know I ought to thank her for driving me home and helping me get in the fashion show. But what I think, not what I say.

"How come you creep 'round Price like you afraid of Miss B?"

Miss Sims don't answer, so I go on talking. "You wanna know what my uncle tell me? He never say it right to disrespect the school people. But he tell me if somebody got a problem and they take their mess out on you, then they not worth the time of day. I listen to my uncle, Miss Sims. That's why Miss B stay away from me. And it don't take words to tell her."

We barreling into Pedro, but I got time to say what's on my mind.

"This is what I don't understand. You know you right. When Miss B come in the theater and mess up our talent show, she not see the good thing you done. She not have the right to do what she did, but you let her do it. That's what I don't understand."

I look over at Miss Sims behind the wheel of her little blue bug. She look sad and I feel bad for what I say. Then she smile and tease me for leaving my shoes at home.

Inside the house, Bettina crawlin on the rug. Miss Sims pick her up and bounce her 'round. I call to Riva.

She come in and give me a look that tell me to clear out fast.

Miss Sims must read the look cause she say to Riva that she got a smart daughter and a beautiful baby.

Riva puff all up and start talking friendly like. I grab the box of shoes by the front door and say we got to go.

On the way back to Price, right before we come to a McDonald's, I tell Miss Sims that I need to eat, what with no lunch. She look at her watch and wing into McDonald's and order a burger and two cokes and don't let me pay. Miss Sims say she wait to drink her coke. I eat my burger too fast and wait on my coke, too.

It already five minutes past the bell when Miss Sims pull into the parking lot. I supposed to report for the fashion show in ten minutes, so I just walk with Miss Sims to her classroom. I got the McDonald's bag with the two cokes and my big purse and the box with the black shoes. Miss Sims see this and take the bag with the cokes, and we walk real fast down the corridor. But turning the corner of the C wing, I look ahead and see Miss B outside Miss Sims' classroom. That's when Miss Sims push the bag with the cokes toward me. I can only think I don't want sticky stuff on my things, so I hesitate. Before I know it, Miss Sims march off toward her room with the bag from Mickey D.

I trail behind her.

Miss B's voice boom down the corridor. "You are eight minutes late, and ..."

Miss B not finish 'cause Miss Sims cut her off. "Mr. Meadows said he would cover my class. He must have forgotten."

Miss B act as if she see me for the first time. "Where are you supposed to be?"

"Goin' to dress for the show."

She say to turn around and get going.

But Miss Sims butt in. "No, I would like Dee Dee to hear this. She had the note from Mr. Meadows."

The classroom door open and I hear no sounds in there. Everybody listening to Miss Sims, who talking in big, round tones.

"There is something I've been meaning to ask you, Miss Braithwine. You treat roses kindly but prune people. Why is that?"

Miss B say nothing. But her look cut you dead.

I think Miss Sims demented to be talking 'bout roses, standing there with the Micky D. bag leaking on her sky blue dress.

But I got other things on my mind.

During the show, the crazy bus girls give out extra loud cheers each time I walk on the stage, the only bus girl to ever be in the show. Riva be proud that I don't make a sound in my black heels, that I keep my chin in the air under the black hat and stride the stage in my white suit like I be Diana Ross or some other famous black singer on TV.

I see Miss B while the models changing in a room behind the stage. She never once look my way, and I think maybe this be the end of it. Maybe she stop bugging Miss Sims. The roses got no meaning for me, but maybe they mean something to Miss B. After the show, Miss Sims come to the room, all smiles.

"Miss B not be bugging you now," I say.

The smile it leave Miss Sim's face. "No, Dee Dee."

"No what?"

The department store lady giving me the eye to get the white suit off.

"Miss B leave you alone. That's my point."

Miss Sims shake her head and say that we gonna talk on Monday 'cause she need my help.

4.

On Monday at the bus stop, I get the feeling that now, after the fashion show, my friends not sure what to make of me. And that morning I find myself not jiving with everybody but staring out the window on the way to Price. I see the same houses on the hill, but they different. The green lawns look like my aunt Lavinia been there, snipping and trimming what unruly. Nobody where we live got lawns that look like they get haircuts and manicures. I sit on the bus, picking at the red polish Lavinia paint on my nails the night before the fashion show. And flicking red flakes off my skirt, I wonder why Miss Sims wanna see me. I hoping she keep it on the sly 'cause it never cool if a teacher act like you somebody special. Then I think that in two weeks I graduate and there be no more Miss B waiting in the parking lot at Price Junior High.

❦

End of second period, Miss Sims slip me a note that say to meet her at lunch, that she buy me a sandwich and to come straight to her room.

Miss Sims got a portable stereo, and on Fridays for free reading she play soft jazz that settle most everybody down. When I get to her room a little after twelve, she over by the stereo, the speakers spread out for use, and she hold a record album in her hands. Before I get close enough to see the face on the cover, Miss Sims begin pumping me with questions. She wanna know what we do on the bus.

I not gonna tell her what I was doing early that day, staring at lawns and thinking one thing and another. So I ask what she mean.

"You, Althea, Portia, Tangee, Kaylah, Lavern ... the whole bunch of you. Do you sit together?"

"Yeah. We sit together in back. Why you ask?"

"Do you ever sing on your long ride?"

"It depend on the driver."

"Does this driver let you sing?"

"He cool. He let us sing."

She making me real curious with her questions.

"Don't say anything about this, Dee Dee. But I won't be at Price next year."

It a sad voice I hear, that make me ask why she leavin' Price.

"Cutbacks. New teachers get cut first. Since you and I won't be at Price next year, this gave me an idea."

She stop talking and go over to her desk and come back with a ham sandwich in a neat little package. She say to go ahead and eat it while we talk. Then Miss Sims walk back and forth in front of the stereo, telling how she come to see Miss B as more than a dean who bug bus kids and new teachers. She say that Miss B bring big bouquets of roses to school and put them on the counter where the teachers sign in. Miss Sims ask the secretary about the flowers and learn that Miss B an expert on roses and even win prizes in flower shows.

Miss Sims lift the stereo arm and put it down real gentle on the turntable. A song begin that I recognize from the radio. Half of my sandwich gone, and I dig out the other half, listening to words 'bout love sweet love ... and lord we don't need another mountain ... and won't you listen Lord ... if you wanna know, if you wanna know. I almost finish the sandwich by the time the song end. And wiping a little mayo from the side of my mouth, I cast a look at the closed door and hope nobody open it and see me there. Miss Sims

64

give me a smile, like it every day she give out a ham sandwich and play a song 'bout love sweet love. Then she flip the album cover over and hold it up.

This is Jackie DeShannon.

That's what the cover say. And the face? Well, it surprise me.

"She be white?"

Miss Sims say that Jackie DeShannon got a gospel, blues sound, and it be perfect for me and my friends.

It then I know that Miss Sims got some crazy plan and in her mind she think I gonna be part of it. I step back, so she see me in full.

"What you cookin' up?"

She start the song over and sing with it this time.

"What the world needs now … is love sweet love … it's the only thing that there's too little of … not just for some … but for everyone."

She lift the arm real careful and ask if I got a record player at home.

"My uncle and aunt live next door. They got a stereo."

Miss Sims say she give me the album so I can teach the lyrics and tune to the bus girls.

I turn and take a real hard look at the door, thinking to make my exit. But Miss Sims go right on talking, as if she got no doubt that I wanna be part of her plan for the grade nine graduate assembly. Well, she got her nerve and I think to tell her so.

Miss Sims give me a long, deep look.

"If you were like everybody else, I wouldn't ask?"

No words come to mind 'cept to say, "Why you wanna do this?"

She say it important to speak a language that a person understand. She ask if I remember the poem we memorize by Langston Hughes.

"Yeah. He that dude from Harlem who write 'bout dreams. I

remember the lines ... I play it cool and dig all jive ... that's the reason I stay alive ... my motto as I live and learn ... is to dig and be dug in return. "

"You didn't miss a word."

" Yeah? Trouble is, Miss Sims ... I don't dig what you tellin' me."

"Maybe not today," she say and give me a big smile.

"Well, it today I got the questions. Where I hide it?"

"Not to worry. My room-mate is tall and has the perfect light weight coat for you to wear."

"Summer comin'. A coat look real dumb."

"You're forgetting June fogs off the Pacific."

She confusing my mind. "But if the bus girls know, how we keep it a secret?"

"They won't know."

"But I teach them the song, they gonna ask when we sing it."

"Tell them to start singing when they hear the call."

"And where the call come from?" I ask all smart-like.

"From the fog ... like a horn."

She messing with my head and it make me mad. The bell ring and Miss Sims say she got to get ready for class. She put the album in my bag, then follow me to the door. When I open it, a searching breeze find a few wisps of her long hair. I let the door slam on my way out.

The day start crazy and it get more so by the hour. I bury the album in my big bag so no bus kid see that cream of wheat face.

5.

The big June day arrive. And as the bus climb the hill to Price, I can't see no lawns cause a mean fog roll in during the night. Me

66

and the bus kids know the Price graduation be different now than before. When busing begin and kids like us come from far away and our families mostly poor, Mr. Meadows change the graduation from a ceremony with fancy dresses for girls and suits for boys, and parents all dressed up, to a short assembly just for students like the one today.

The girls been singing the song to and from school, and everybody on the bus sick of it. The bus driver keep asking if that be the only song we know. And Willy and Tony keep telling us we crazy and demented.

I meet Miss Sims before school and it then she tell me what to do. The teachers get the program in their boxes that morning. The choir gonna sing a bunch of songs, the best girl and boy graduate speak, then counselors read the names of the honor roll, and finally the two deans get to talk. Miss B the last one before Mr. Meadows hand out diplomas. Miss Sims tell me when Miss Braithwine take the microphone and say her first word, that's when I suppose to rise and head up the aisle.

"When do I get ..."

She know my question and say to stash my big bag in my locker, then meet in the homemaking room right before the assembly.

I keep listening but inside it all a dream. The classes get cut short our last day at Price, with only enough time to get our grade cards and listen like always to the teachers. At the ten-minute break, I remind the bus girls to sit together.

"But we be made to sit with our Homeroom," Portia say. "Some of us got one room. Some got the other."

"What they gonna do, Portia? You graduate today."

When the bell it ring for assembly, I find Miss Sims outside the homemaking room with a long tan coat over her arm. The sun not peeking from the fog so maybe I not look too funny wearing a coat. Once we get inside the room, Miss Sims open the refrigerator there. What she hand me bigger than I think it gonna be, but we hide it under the coat and with my hand in the pocket I put enough pressure on one end to keep it in place. I so skinny that nobody see the bulge.

"Sit in the very back," she say.

"What if they don't start singin', Miss Sims?"

"They will." With that she give me a nudge. I walk out the door and don't look back. I pass by the stage that I stroll on just two weeks before, and I find a seat on the aisle in the last row and slump down so nobody pay me no mind.

I sit through the choir singing and the best boy and girl graduate talking.

Then everybody get to hear from the counselors, Mrs. Smith and Mr. Carver.

Next Mr. Dicks head to the microphone.

When he finish, Miss Braithwine stand to make her way to the center of the stage. Her glasses shine a little 'cause the sun burn off the fog. Miss B take hold of the microphone and her first word it ring out. "Today ..."

And today not a dream 'cause I stand, all six feet of me, and with my open coat flapping, I take off fast for the stage, worried that some teacher try to stop me, though it not like I toting a gun. In my hands I got long stem red roses wrapped in crinkling cellophane, so all their glory red march right on through for everybody to see. Even though I move fast up the aisle, time seem to stop 'cause everybody staring at me. It then, wherever Miss Sims be, I wanna knock her head so she never forget me. But when I get halfway to the stage, part of one row rise. Miss Sims be right after all. The bus girls hear the call, and they got arms locked together, singing real faint at first 'bout the world needin' love sweet love. Then the singing rise in volume 'cause every idiot on the bus singing, too.

I climb the steps to the stage and stop in front of Miss B. But her body look as frozen as her mouth. I hold out the roses but she don't take 'em. I stand for what feel like forever with my long arms outstretched toward Miss B, and if a look kill, then I be dead. But the music get louder and louder 'cause white kids at Price singing, too.

Mr. Meadows stand, slow like always, and he come forward and he take the roses, and he give them to Miss B. The smile in his face and the tears in his eyes be something I never forget. It then I fly off that stage and make a hundred yard dash for the gym on the far side of Price, not giving a rat's ass if I get my diploma or not.

Miss B got no tears. But her one word no longer sound in the open air. Today been drowned out by the song still being sung.

I wait a long time in the gym locker room till I know the buses leave and the white kids go home and the halls be empty.

Then I walk to Miss Sims room and stand at the door, watching her clear out a cupboard. When I speak, she turn round and see me.

"How come you buy roses that got no thorns?"

Miss Sims start laughing, wild and free, like the day she call me the black widow.

I can laugh about this now … writing these words eighteen years later in my office at Stein Brothers.

But it hard to say good-bye that day. Miss Sims offer me a ride home. But I tell her a long walk and a San Pedro city bus feel right for the last day at Price. She give me my diploma, then we talk a while, till I know it time to start down the hill.

Miss Sims take my hands in hers and she look in my eyes. "I will never forget you or this day, Dee Dee."

I got no words to give, just purse my lips, so as not to cry.

But all these years later, Miss Sims not gone from my mind, and that lead me to believe I not gone from hers either.

Whenever I get clogged, start feeling low, don't see where life lead, then I remember what happen between Miss Sims and Miss B and me, and the memory bring back my spirit. And then I know, I just as deadly as ever.

As Deadly as Ever
2020 NLAPW Biennial/Letters Competition
Middle School Story Award, 1st Place
Judge: Sandra Seaton Michel

Non-Fiction

Ms. Smith-Corona

Soon after my family moved to West Germany in 1980, a letter arrived in the tiny village of Otterberg. New Reader's Press was asking me to send the book I'd proposed months earlier and, based on the four chapters I'd submitted, the company wanted to publish the fictional account of my great-great grandfather's 1849 journey from Vermont to California. Time, however, was of the essence. New Reader's Press had to have the completed book within the next six to eight weeks.

No matter how much time I had in those days with small children, the hours were never enough. And we were living in a country where we and our appliances didn't feel at home. In this new land of 230/50 electricity, everything from the mix master to the stereo felt disturbed by life in West Germany. My electric typewriter, in particular, had begun to rebel, smoking its way through the morning, decidedly pissed off about the transformer, an unwanted mate: a gray, 10-inch square metal thing, weighing at least eight pounds if not more. But I whispered to Ms. Smith-Corona to think about our good news, telling her we could have a book with our name on the cover, a book to help adults who couldn't read, a book to help immigrants learn English, a book about leaving home and feeling lost, which is how I felt in West Germany. An English teacher and a writer, I loved words, but now found myself wordless in a small village where most residents spoke only German.

Unfortunately, my faithful electric typewriter didn't share my enthusiasm for the possibility of a published epistolary novel; and a few days later, Ms. Smith-Corona impolitely froze up. No more dissenting sounds and smells. Only her silence. Buy a new one, I thought— an electric typewriter that can be plugged directly into the socket, not into that noisy transformer, a typewriter that purrs contently on 50 cycles. My husband, an Air Force major, agreed with my plan because the letter from New Reader's Press stated that I would be paid for writing the book and given annual royalties.

The following evening, Mike returned from the base with 400 dollars in *Deutsch* marks. He showed me the money but wouldn't hand it over until he played commander, which he was of a squadron.

"Do not leave the store tomorrow without the paper for the *Marastoya*."

I couldn't spell or correctly pronounce the German word, but I knew it meant getting 18% of the purchase price back from the German government through the U.S. military.

The following morning, I got first grader Michelle on the bus to Sembach Air Force base and walked Bonnie, age three, to German kindergarten in the village. Then I dashed home and headed for Kaiserslautern, tearing through the village of Otterberg in my black Volkswagen Rabbit, only not driving too quickly because the day before I'd been stopped just outside the city limits. Two German policemen had displayed obvious delight to ticket an American *Frau* who couldn't argue with them in German. Once again on this day, I saw the same two men and waved, cheerfully intent on getting to Masse, the Wallmart of Germany.

The electric typewriter in the mega-store looked identical to the one I'd burned up, right down to its color of robin egg blue.

Forget the *Marastoya*, I thought, dreading the oppressive feeling of being wordless, as if the god of intellect had feasted on my brain. But I couldn't ignore my husband's order. And no doubt because the cashier had checked out countless mute Americans, she intuited that I was not paying for the typewriter until I had the tax paper for it. When I repeated, "paper," she pointed to an office on the second floor, visible through large glass windows that overlooked the Masse of Kaiserslautern.

Upstairs I entered an orderly room where some twenty women were lined up at typewriters. At 38 I still looked young, the dismissive treatment of old age having not yet begun. My smile felt forced, however, because I resembled a slovenly American that morning. Rule number one *then*, for kinder treatment in Germany: Wear decent clothing. Rule number two: Wash and wax your car. Rule number three: Use appliances for 230/50. Even though I was wordless and poorly clad, my goal was steadfast—to get the tax paper and quickly finish the book for New Reader's Press.

"*Die papel*," I said to the woman whose desk was separate from the pool of typists. Was that even the word? Half of it had the ring of *paper* in Spanish.

The matron's sullen face registered only boredom. I'd had menial jobs, knew all about long days at a typewriter, clicking life away. Looking more closely around the room, I saw that the clerks came in all ages and shapes.

"*Paper!*" I said loudly, dropping the *die, der, das* bit, which had given me a new appreciation for *the* in English.

"Paper, *bitte*," I said a third time, adding *please*.

Keys ceased typing in the room, and German leapt from mouths, along with cackling. I heard someone say, "*Dummkopf.*" I understood the word. Children shouted it at Michelle and Bonnie on the village playground. Suddenly the English word I'd spoken rippled from mouths throughout the room.

"Paper? For the toilet?" one typist asked. The cackling erupted again. Then a woman with long blond hair stood and stared at the woman who had spoken in English. Most of the women dropped their heads, started moving their fingers again. The blond approached me, said she was married to an American soldier, knew what I was after. She led me to another desk, told that woman what to do, and kindly explained in English what she had said, and returned to her desk in the now busy room.

The clerk typed a form, which had to be signed. Under the line for my name, I saw what she had typed? *Frau* Smith-Corona. I found this marvelously funny. Yet I had no way to share the joke with those in the room. *Don't you see? In one way or another, we're all ignorant.* All I could do, however, was point to my German driver's license. The clerk saw the correct name, shrugged, and retyped the form.

The drive home felt short because a smug feeling replaced my wordless stupidity I'd felt at Masse. Yes, *indeed*. I was going to bang out a book on my new electric typewriter in the next few weeks. And once inside our tiny apartment, I lifted the typewriter from its box and plugged in the lovely robin-egg blue Smith-Corona and listened to its welcome purr. I rolled in a sheet of paper, inserted one of the cartridges from my old Smith-Corona, touched the new keys with glee, and typed a few words before glancing at them. That's when I shouted an obscenity, one easily said in German because it is similar to the English.

Swearing only intensified my frustration, and anger brought tears, which wet the German keyboard in our tiny apartment where there was not all the time in the world to rewire my brain so I could type on this new and unfamiliar keyboard, with its vowels where they had never been before and would never be again after we left West Germany three years later. And saying the only correct German word I truly knew and understood, I repeated it to the power of three ... *dummkopf, dummkopf, dummkopf.*

Ms. Smith-Corona
Memoir Vignette, Honorable Mention, 2016
Judge: Linda Joy Myers

Humbled by a Roach

During my twenties it was mice, scrambling across the attic, or peering from kitchen drawers. Mice were annoying. But using tongs I tossed them, along with their mouse traps, out the backdoor into the field behind the tiny house I rented while my husband flew that year in Thailand. Then in my thirties, tree rats invaded the old house we bought in California's Napa Valley. Rats were more menacing than mice but met their end in large traps. Then in my late thirties we moved to a small, rural village in West Germany. There it was big, nasty, aggressive 'horse' flies. Yet armed with a fly swatter, I took on the Messerschmitt of the fly corps. When I turned 40, we returned to California. The German flies had made me forget about ants. I stuck a jar of honey in a cupboard and, before I ever saw then, I knew a large company of ants had marched in. Two years later we moved again, to the South, and nothing—not mice, rats, flies, or ants have affected me the way cockroaches did in Montgomery, Alabama.

As a writer I keep strange hours. At Air Force University, I realized we were sharing 1940 era quarters with cockroaches. Imagine my shock when I discovered a roach sucking on my toothbrush one night. At 4 a.m., a two-inch cockroach looks bigger and bolder than in daylight. Having pulverized vermin in the past, I reacted as I always had. But damned if I could defeat a cockroach! It was this creature's eating habits and shrewd getaways that aroused my curiosity.

"Disgusting," my daughters said when I returned home with library books about roaches. Bring home books on pandas and kids coo with delight. While the poor panda depends on bamboo for its survival, a roach is not fussy. It can eat paint off the wall and grow bigger and bolder on something that in earlier times gave humans lead poisoning.

My respect for cockroaches as survivors made me start observing them. I do not wish to imply they ceased to startle me when I heard their crackling exits across my anti-roach shelf liner. Yet my behavior with cockroaches changed. Whenever one crept into view, I watched it. That was how I came to appreciate the antennae that pivot so gracefully on a roach's head; and I marveled that roaches easily slip into crevices far too small for them. One night I imagined myself as a cockroach, as if I were Gregor Samsa in Franz Kafka's *The Metamorphosis*, only smaller. I knew if I saw a human, I would freeze in fright. Yet my record of success with cockroaches was dismal. By the time I raised my hand or lifted a foot, the roach received a message from its rear feelers and fled.

From learning about cockroaches, I concluded humans more closely resemble moths, as Virginia Woolf wrote long ago. Humanity keeps doing dumb things, even when stakes have reached cataclysmic proportions on planet earth. But the roach is not learning disabled. Shock a roach and it gets the message, while a moth heads for the flame.

There is so much to admire about cockroaches. They can be frozen and thawed. (Good trait for an ice age.) They need little oxygen and can handle gobs of radiation. (Handy attribute in the nuclear age.) And if you poison roaches, they adapt, which means this creature will no doubt bid adieu to computers, the same way it waved good-bye to dinosaurs.

Yet instead of tipping our hats, we give the cockroach bad press. I recall a front-page article in *The Washington Post* about an invasion of Asian cockroaches. In the reporter's opening paragraph, he used the words, "repulsive, obnoxious, and offensive" to describe this ancient creature. Contrast his attitude to a curator at the Smithsonian's Insect Zoo. "They know I'm their friend," he told me, "so they no longer hiss. Here, pet one," he said, reaching in his pocket for one of the many cockroaches he had with him that day in Washington, D.C. When I told him about my family's upcoming move to Malaysia, he said to expect six-inch cockroaches there, adding facts I had not read about roaches. They can live without a head, go through several molts, and use their old skin as a source of nutrition. "Imagine if we could do that with adipose?" the curator laughed. I left the Natural Science Museum more humbled than ever.

Later, when I read the State Department report on Malaysia, it mentioned two diseases from mosquitoes: dengue and malaria. Since childhood, mosquitoes have been attracted to my blood. Not to worry! In Kuala Lumpur, the health ministry regularly smoked our neighborhood to kill mosquitoes, and the geckoes who lived in our house ate mosquitos that escaped the smoke. Plus, an exterminator made regular calls to take care of mice and bugs too hefty for geckoes. The cobras, plentiful alongside the nearby Royal Selangor golf course, were the gardener's responsibility, for which he was well paid for his vigilance.

I will skip the decade in Venezuela, Colombia, and Peru. Who could worry about vermin in countries with *golpe de estados* (remember Hugo Chavez), FARC guerillas in Colombia, *Sendero Luminoso* and MRTA revolutionaries in Peru? Instead, I will end in the Northern Neck of Virginia, where I've spent the last fifteen years, living on a creek of the Chesapeake Bay.

I knew thick woods would mean numerous creatures—the whole panoply of the past: mice, rats, horse flies, ants, mosquitoes, plus copperheads to replace cobras. At present no cockroaches; and with their absence I seem to have forgotten how they humbled me in the past. And really, I ought to be mortified when my pubescent grandson awakens, opens the back door, shouts "Spider patrol," and begins knocking large spiders off the walls, replicating his Nana's non-Buddhist behavior.

Yes, sadly, I have regressed and found a new enemy, something I knew in childhood as Granddaddy Longlegs. Not really a spider. And the ones here have no charm like their California cousins. Why have these creatures so unsettled me and brought forth my worst human traits in nature's world of dappled creatures? Our cottage and the house built later are planked with Hardy board, now covered with what a painter recently identified as "spider shit." SS I will call it to sound more gentile. I heard the painter's words and hung my head, literally. I had accused my husband during the years we lived in the cottage and had no oven and used only the barbecue, of incinerating swarms of no-see-ums, which in death adhered like glue to the plank. Careful observation validated the painter's alliterative SS. I know the subject is distasteful. But so is squashing this creature and discovering its essence, its veritable core, is a pocket of black goo impervious to power washing or the direct application of any number of strong cleaners.

It's all metaphorical, isn't it, by the seventh decade of life? The fighting of decay, the battling against nature's progression: acne to wrinkles, exploding brain cells to diminishing ones, quick feet to unwelcome tumbles, jiggling flesh to scattered ashes. The English writer, Julian Barnes, in his treatise on death (*Nothing to Be Frightened Of*) states that irony does not dry up the grass—it just burns off the weeds. If this is true, does it mean that in another decade, if I have not blown away in my eighties, that I will have evolved a lust for dappled and unspotted creatures; that I will love nature's contagion; that I will thank the pseudo spiders for choosing my house as their place of excrement; and that in my enlightenment, I will be addressed on Mill Creek Lane in rural Virginia, as Oh, Dolly Lama?

Seriously? Considering my past behavior with God's dappled creatures, isn't the likelihood that my departure on life's stage will not be as Oh, Dolly Lama but *Auntie Mame*? Or as the role relates to me, Auntie Maimed?

Humbled by a Roach
Humor, 2nd Place, 2015
Judge: Jamie Cat Callan

Ink-Stained Wench

Here in the backwoods of Virginia in my declining years, why not reveal my *deal* upfront, even though I dislike cards, a hangover from childhood when I had to play poker and Canasta with my parents and brother. Poker's strip variety came later in college with a bit more attraction than cards with Mom and Dad. Yet from the day I could turn pages and make sense of words, I wanted to read books — not shuffle cards. So, what's my deal? I'm thought to be more educated and intelligent than I am. The fluency gained from being a voracious reader can give this impression. My love of reading also led me to think I might write. Yet before I could seriously consider writing I had to overcome the Shakespeare Syndrome. This is a belief that it's folly to write without an innate genius like Virginia Woolf's, or the talent to belt whiskey and words like William Faulkner in Old Miss. Still, after concluding that writing wouldn't cost me anything except time, paper, and postage, I plunged in.

What I initially created with words shared a resemblance to sausage. Even I was not sure what had been ground up, stuffed into a thin skin, with the content pulverized from years of copious reading. Yet with experience and changing times, my writing took on the appearance of an egg roll: fried outside, lots of bean sprouts, tiny pieces of pork — or if my readers were vegetarian, eggs instead of meat. Sadly, I've yet to produce a four-star Michelin essay. Chefs kill for this award, it's said. Not the cooks at racially suspect Henny's (as I'll call it). This is relevant because I count on my readers to be Henny diners: waking from a *siesta*, gummy-eyed from dreaming about dinner, not concerned with substance or details, fooled by verbal offal (no irony that awful and offal rhyme, at least to my defective ear.) This too is part of my deal, that awful/offal cliché about getting a bad deck of cards, without the jokers for talent and genius. I must add that four years of living in Venezuela taught me this: The cliché about getting a bad deck applies to countries as well as to individuals. Venezuela at present is tragically imploding. Yet for over four stressful years, I pole vaulted the highways of this surreal and chaotic country.

No pole vaulting now. What's ahead is a cane that never leaves the ground, tapping down Decrepitude Lane.

Living in ol' Virginy, I try to remember the days when I was sprinting in the world. Overcome by nostalgia the other day, I put on a CD and listened to Bob Dylan singing, "Just Like a Woman," and thought about how he won the Nobel Prize in Literature. Still perplexed by the Nobel Committee's decision to award Dylan this prize, I listened to "Desolation Row," recalling how I'd described my early writing as a sausage. It's remarkable how many borrowed names Dylan stuffed into this one song about desolation: Cinderella, Robin Hood, Casanova, Phantom of the Opera, Hunchback of Notre Dame, plus the usual Biblical borrowings like Noah, Cain and Abel, and the Good Samaritan. Who today easily recognizes Dylan's references to T.S. Eliot and Ophelia?

Sorry, I've again digressed.

Here's the current deal.

If I had to come up with a metaphor that fits life now, it would have nothing to do with cards. It would be ink-stained wench.

My husband (the same one for over 50 years) recently called me this. Until retirement, he spent his life serving the Air Force, State Department, and United Nations. This means he sat through innumerable sensitivity training sessions and learned to avoid using words that reflect 'ism' thinking. Unlike what I might say to Donald Trump, I do not accuse my husband of overt sexism. I would argue, however, that like most men, he inherited misogyny as a blood type. My husband is the proud father of two gutsy, independent daughters. The older is a colonel in the U.S. Army, recently commanded a brigade of 3500 soldiers in Germany. Her younger sister has been an NGO abroad, traveling by bus in places that few tourists visit, such as Tamil territory in Sri Lanka, rural India, and Laos. My husband is a good father to our daughters, and they know him as a man who does not spew epithets at women. They see their father as a helpful pragmatist: a pilot who flew airplanes for most of his life, commanded maintenance squadrons for that big bird the C-5, directed the aerial eradication of coca and poppy (cocaine & heroin) in Colombia, and managed food relief flights in Banda Aceh, Indonesia, after the 2004 tsunami. This good man has been a giver, not one of those rich-boy takers in life.

So exactly what caused my husband to fling an insulting word of dubious origins at me one morning? I heard the word and flew into my study, adjacent to our bedroom. There I consulted my unabridged Oxford dictionary. It provided a list through the centuries for wench: girl, working-class girl, servant, licentious woman, prostitute, and mistress. In 1200, the word referred to a small child of the female sex (inaccurate for me, considering my age and the fact that I call myself a woman.) But it is accurate to say that I've often regarded myself as a servant girl, which wench came to mean by the late 1500s. And lurking in this word's background since the 1300s is the connotation of a wanton woman, and man as wench, the consort of licentious women.

Armed with this ethno-linguistic knowledge, I was ready to

launch a battle with my husband for having used *wench* to describe me. But here's the rub, borrowing a phrase from Elizabethan Willy the Shake. My husband qualified *wench* with ink-stained. The final straw, to use an old saw, had made him swear at me. And ink-stained referred to the condition of our queen-sized bed, not to mention the brand new, pale yellow sheets, and the mattress pad beneath them. All were smeared with black ink, the result of the pen I'd held when I fell asleep.

During the night I must have *wrenched* every which way to dislodge that much ink from a Uniball Vision Elite, the new BLX, black ink infused with colors. It is advertised as "airplane safe-ink" that "will not explode or leak due to a change in cabin pressure during flights." These words can be read on any ten-pack of Uniball Vision Elite pens, which I purchase in bulk to help defray the expense of going through so much ink. And from frequent travel, I can state with assurance that a Uniball Vision Elite will not leak on an airplane in flight. Sadly, this is not true for sea-level beds.

The ruined sheets were one thing. But my new nightgown, a gift from my husband for cold winters in Virginia, had been worn only once: a long soft gown scattered with red cardinals, the same birds that remain in our garden all winter, delighting us with their vibrant red and orange feathers. My nightgown, once as white as snow, on which cardinals cavorted, was now a patchwork of black ink infused with the hue of purple's passion, a sight that blew my husband's marital fuse. "Fifty years of your damn pens in our bed, you ink-stained wench!"

That same morning, husband Mike returned from tiny Kilmarnock with a pencil sharpener and a box of twelve yellow pencils. Being by nature a kind man, he spared me a litany of how many sets of sheets I'd ruined through the years, from double to queen to king. And he didn't mention the hotels where I've left my 'Kilroy's mistress was here'. Nor did he remind me of the umbrage I've caused an obsessive-compulsive relative who has found my ink on various bedspreads and sheets in his houses.

There we were, my husband and I, with the pencil sharpener and a box of pencils on the kitchen counter. He was tapping an index and middle finger on the granite, waiting to hear what I would say about his purchase. I ran a few delusional thoughts through my mind, such as black sheets and black pajamas. Strangely, this death-like image made me think of the late John Updike. At the time of Updike's death, his *review* copies of novels with his witty and wicked comments on almost every page had fetched a high price at auction. I said this tidbit to Mike, adding, "What would the books have been worth if Updike had written in pencil?"

"You're not Updike," he said unkindly, as if I had the delusion of being a transgender literary great.

"Underlining books was how Updike prayed," I said, hoping one little word of religious action might soften my husband's Catholic heart regarding ink pens in our bed.

He gave me his most skeptical look. "You, the agnostic, are invoking religion in your defense?"

"Mike," I said, "I do not doubt God as a probability. But pencil erasure? That's a damn certainty."

"Here," he said, handing me the pencil sharpener. "Keep it on your desk."

This of course is not where the story ends.

The truth is that from my hands I have not *wrenched* any real means of subsistence from writing. For my husband, 1950s fellow that he is, success has an economic component. Often, I have quoted Joseph Conrad's, "In art there is meaning apart from success." I once used Arial in 22 font to reproduce Conrad's quote, which I attached to the bulletin board beside my desk, along with another quote I'd memorized in *my* (unmarried) *salad days when I was green in judgment.* (Thank you William Shakespeare, for this brilliant phrase.)

The quote was from the writer, Francine Du Plessix Gray, whose words I added to the board. She wrote that, "Marriage is the utterly necessary compromise between occasional bliss and terminal boredom." When my husband read the quote, he told me the bliss had been occasional because I preferred reading to sex. That wasn't always true and certainly not in my salad days.

Yet determined to make it to our 51st anniversary, I now keep sharpened pencils by the bed, alongside whatever book I'm currently reading. This month it happens to be *Don Quixote* at a hefty 900 pages. I love every word that Cervantes whispers in my ear, as translated into English in a new edition by the brilliant Edith Grossman. And located near the famous tale of a Knight's long journey are vials of Restasis for dry-eye, and three plastic molds worn at night on three fingers of my right hand. Apparently, my misshapen, arthritic fingers are the result of holding pens much too tightly for so many decades.

Dare I admit to my reader that there is a hidden Uniball Vision Elite on the night stand, too? The pen's presence helps me maintain a hope that one day I will write a four-star essay, and that my husband will pay for an award-winning meal. I already know the money earned from my writing will not be enough for the Senior Special at Henny's. Do I despair? No, and for one simple reason. In art there is meaning greater than economic success.

Ink-Stained Wench
Humor, 1st Place, 2016
Judge: Jamie Cat Callan

Sisyphus on Crosshills

On the Virginia roadway I've adopted in memory of my father, I'm keenly aware of how ambivalent Father would be about his daughter picking up trash. The word resonated with him, related to a place and a time he did not easily call his own. Too many years of Dust Bowl refugees flooding California, cinematic images of *The Grapes of Wrath*, and words like Okies. I don't recall a time during my California youth when Father talked openly about being from Arkansas.

Odd memories come to me as I collect litter in the Northern Neck of Virginia on Route 679, known as Crosshills. The first time I traveled this road in 2004, I loved it. First, passing open farmland, then entering a mysterious tree-canopied stretch that ends on Ball's Neck, Route 605. One morning, after the V-DOT adoption was complete, I walked beneath trees on Crosshills with a bulging thirty-gallon, orange trash bag in hand. Strange the way memories come to us. Suddenly I recalled a night during my graduate days in San Francisco, when in an elegant restaurant, my date began eating a Caesar salad with his fingers, leaf by dripping leaf. Seeing my expression of disbelief, this wealthy young man said, "If you know who you are, you can eat however you like."

Such privileged insouciance was not my father's birthright. He never shed an old coat of the rural, segregated South, and the unease of ever being thought 'white trash'. As a young man living in southern California in the late 1920s, Robert Wilson went to college on a basketball scholarship to a university for rich kids. In a photo at the University of Southern California, my father is surrounded by handsome young men from his fraternity house, all elegantly dressed like Gatsby in West Egg finery, with sweaters tossed over their shoulders. My father's sweater looks ill-shaped and appears to have a hole in one sleeve.

Another day as I collected trash on Crosshills, a former student came to mind from a class I student taught outside San Francisco in 1966. A year later, following her high school graduation, Sue surprised me in Redondo Beach, arriving in Haight-Ashbury attire, with a stash of pot in her backpack. At the time she was visiting her sister who lived in southern California. But what was the probability of running into my father in a tiny Mexican restaurant in Palos Verdes? Mother was away at the time, and Father had gone out to eat. Sue and I were already in a booth when I saw him sit down at the counter. I assumed at some point he would swivel on the stool and see me. So, I walked over and invited him to join us. Sue, not trusting anyone over 30, sat there as if stoned. My memory of that meal is a dry, bean burrito stuck in my throat. Later Father said he hadn't paid for my expensive education so I could rescue "street people."

Recently, a neighbor stopped while I was gathering litter on Crosshills. "They'll throw trash just to spite you," he called out, without identifying they. Shortly after he said this, someone sprayed angry epithets on several adopt-a-highway signs on 200, a main road to nearby Kilmarnock.

Hostility seems women into littering. To open a car window and toss the remains of a meal, right down to the tiny packets of pepper and salt: Can this be unconscious behavior? Often on my adopted roadway, people dump household garbage, old tires, and automotive parts. Once I found a rusted wheelbarrow and hauled that to the county dump. As I gather trash, there is no accounting for the images that come to mind. Alice's Restaurant? Didn't Arlo Guthrie's film character get arrested because his litter was found in a dumpster where it didn't belong? This memory led to a fantasy of finding evidence that would identify a litterbug. Although what my action would be was not clear until I came across several envelopes from the Department of Labor, addressed to a man whose post office box was a row away from mine. I wrote Clarence a note, returned his several envelopes, said I hoped he hadn't meant to leave his mail on Crosshills.

One aging woman.

One long stretch of roadway in a county and a country strewn with trash.

Sisyphean.

The word came to me one day when my neighbor stopped a second time and called to me. "You'll be doing that forever," he said. It was his comment that made me think of Sisyphus, whose punishment in Hades was to roll a boulder uphill, eternally. Sisyphean: endless, heart-breaking work. Accounts vary as to Sisyphus's misdeeds, but one unrelated fact is evident to me. My behavior with Father was often adolescent, not unlike the actions of those who toss trash to spite those who pick it up.

Like my father, I've led a migratory life, absorbing traditions of other cultures. By the time I moved to Malaysia in the late 80s, Father was dead; and I regretted deeply that I'd not asked him more about his work in Asia for Sunkist Growers. Even though I was in California to attend Father's memorial service, I was not there when Mother spread his ashes among their avocado trees. Yet from living in Asia among the Chinese, I had observed the practice of ancestral shrines, of creating a place to honor ancestors. For Robert Theron Wilson, an ancestral shrine had to be outdoors, as nature was his religion. A storm could wipe out his avocado crop. Yet he accepted the devastation and economic loss with a stoical attitude I admire.

Now.

For many seniors, memory is a litter that exhibits a worrisome tendency to live in the past. My father, however, relished old stories of his foreign travel, which began during college at USC when he took a year off and worked on a tramp steamer for free passage to Europe. In a small journal, he recorded his adventures of traveling around the continent in the early 1930s. Decades later, when Sunkist Growers began exporting fruit to Europe and later to Asia, Father spent long periods abroad. He even devised the system for pallets that kept exported citrus from spoilage.

One day last winter, as I traversed a barren Crosshills beneath denuded trees, I thought of a last walk with my father. He and my mother had driven to Vacaville, California, following Father's open-heart surgery in 1983. As he and I walked in an area of new homes, I noticed he was shuffling. It was the only way I knew how weak he was from the operation. Although he rallied, Father soon began to decline. His surgery was before the widespread news about AIDS. I picture a desperate soul, a drug user or prostitute, selling his or her blood in San Diego. No testing of blood in 1983 for HIV. Two years later, was it AIDS that took my father's life? My mother's request for an autopsy was not granted. She had wanted to know why her husband recovered from surgery, then fell into a lethargy so deep he could not get up to work on the ranch. There were strange lesions on his body, too. Eventually hospitalized with an infected lining of the heart, he wasn't treated with antibiotics, as if his death were a foregone conclusion. He died alone in a hospital in Escondido, with my mother having left for the night. My brother was not there either. And I was away in Germany with my husband and two children.

As I walk my stretch of scenic Virginia Byway that bears my father's name on four signs, I think about his final moments and what it means to die alone. Recently, I heard an interview with the British author, Julian Barnes, and I took note of something he said. Until his late thirties he had seldom thought about death. But after he turned forty, he couldn't believe he had ever thought of anything else. Unlike this writer, I began thinking about death early in life, which is why I found comfort in the eternal motion of waves as I wandered the shore in early morning at Newport Beach, where my family spent two weeks each June. Enchanted by foam and spume, and sand bars on which I could walk out into the Pacific, I also began noticing flotsam and jetsam, and the seagulls diving into it. Today, when I see advertisements for cruise ships, I think about their waste polluting oceans. In my childhood, ships dumped garbage at sea, which high tide distributed, and low tide revealed: orange peels, celery stalks, tin cans, and a residue of tar that stuck to bare feet.

Have I been noticing trash my entire life?

"Hey, bag lady," another neighbor called out recently. For ten years this woman's church adopted Crosshills. She speaks of the experience unfavorably. It was hard to recruit help, she told me. But more than that, *they* would throw trash even as she and other volunteers picked it up. Recalling her words, I recognize how easy it would be to debase those who heave trash and garbage on roadways. Yet in the Northern Neck, I'm finding claimants of "they'll throw trash just to spite you," not unlike U.S. Embassy personnel in Caracas, who expressed dismay that I worked with incarcerated North Americans, all of whom were imprisoned on drug-related charges. Mules, scum bags: I heard these words often. But the stereotypes of drug users seldom held truth about individuals; and this memory serves to remind me not to judge those who litter. Yet I can count on two hands the water bottles I've found while beer bottles number in the hundreds! Thus far on Crosshills, I haven't come across any dead animals. I mention this because the other day, I read an interview with the writer, Barry Lopez, who described removing dead animals from roadways as a gesture of kindness, so cars will not hit the creatures that feed on carrion. Through this action, Lopez believes a person honors both the animal and nature.

In his years after retirement, when my father owned a small ranch in California's Pauma Valley, he religiously fed quail, waiting each evening at dusk for a covey to come in. Only now at seventy, have I begun to understand why Father patiently sat and watched quail. In so many ways, he and I are alike: our impatience with pretense, our need to tell stories whether anyone wants to hear them or not; and at the end of a thin stretch of time, Robert Theron Wilson and his only daughter, pleased to feed birds, relish sunsets, and wade in tides of memory.

"I have had to learn the simplest things last, which made for difficulties," the poet Charles Olson wrote.

Driving past corn and soybean fields in the Northern Neck of Virginia, I like to sing "My Way" with the soulful, foot-stomping, Spanish-singing Gipsy Kings. Regrets, I've had a few. One is that my father read only one of my books, a short work used in ESL and adult literacy, a book that fictionalized my great-great grand-father's 1949 Gold Rush letters, written enroute to California, when Eugene Chase went West with the Pioneer Line. He returned home to the East by sea. Father pointed out that I had mistaken Cape Hope for Cape Horn. That was it. He wasn't a man to heap praise on me, which means I feel no need for drivers to stop and thank me for removing trash from Crosshills. I do this because it's Sisyphean: climbing to descend, then climbing again, struggling to be just a bit kinder and wiser in the years that remain.

All is still this Sunday morning, as I listen to Gregorian Chants and look at the marshlands of Mill Creek. The last piece I wrote for money was on a Peruvian potter. The artist, Carlos Runcie Tanaka, loved it, as did I, until the editor left changes on every page, having misunderstood so much about the artist I had portrayed. "Forget the commercial world," a writer-friend recently told me. "Write to make discoveries."

Hearing her words, I ask myself: What are the fragments for if not to be rejoined? So here I sit, an archeologist of the spirit, digging into the past, fingers in a remembered desert, trying to reshape an urn, studying rediscovered pieces to see how they fit together. How very different from finding tiny liquor bottles in paper sacks, and the remains of fast food, right down to unused packets of catsup: Modern trash, not ancient earthen vessels. Yet to discover who you are, what formed you, what shape fragments have given to life: This is what I seek as I traverse the miles on Crosshills, between signs that say, In Memory of Robert T. Wilson.

Sisyphus on Crosshills
Creative Nonfiction, 2nd Place, 2012
Judge: Katheryn Krotzer Laborde

Malay Days/Separation

The names resound, spoken on television and seen on screens — of terrorist attacks in Paris, Brussels, Istanbul, Baghdad, Dhaka, and even U.S. cities. I write the names and think back to 1986 at Air University in Montgomery, Alabama, and the course I audited because I knew so little about the Muslim world.

In *The Political Structure of Islam,* I was the only military spouse among the twelve officers from the U.S. and other countries. A Saudi prince/colonel sat beside the professor at his table in front of the room, as if he required separation from students seated at the other tables. Two Israeli Air Force colonels sat to the right of me, and although we didn't have assigned seats, everyone took the same places each week. The prince always arrived with a stack of books and thumbed through them during class. Our instructor, a noted scholar of Middle East politics, on sabbatical from the Ivy League to Air University for the year, had been in the Peace Corps in North Africa and spoke fluent Arabic. In class he covered vast amounts of material and didn't engage our opinions. The Saudi prince, however, often interrupted a lecture. One day his stack of books included *The Protocols of the Elders of Zion,* which he began quoting. In a stern voice, the professor said, "I will not listen to a Jew conspiracy theory of history."

The following year in August of 1987, my family moved to Malaysia for my husband's posting at the U.S. Embassy. Just down the street from our residence in Kuala Lumpur was the Palestine Liberation Organization (PLO). Shortly after arriving in country, my daughters and I watched the world-wide televised Miss Universe contest, broadcast in English. To our surprise, one contestant of the ten semi-finalists was a blur on the screen. Malaysian state-controlled television could not allow Miss Israel to be seen. After all, the country she represented did not officially exist. My daughters in eighth and fifth grades didn't understand. I'd just visited Israel to see a good friend, and I explained to the girls that the Malaysian government denied entrance to anyone with an Israeli stamp in their passport. That's why I had requested a stamp printed on paper, which I removed from my passport after I left Israel, so I wouldn't be prohibited from entering Malaysia or other Muslim countries.

Within a month of arriving in country, I interviewed for a teaching position with the University of Maryland, then learned the program had been ordered to leave—a departure related to an American professor's comments about Israel, a country that Malaysian students did not see on maps studied in school. Maryland's provost forwarded my application to Indiana University's campus, not far from Kuala Lumpur.

Landing the position with Indiana was one of fortuitous timing. My application reached the provost's desk the same day a delegation of Malay students demanded that they be given another professor for their English 131 composition class. (An action uncharacteristic of Malay students as I came to know them.) It turned out the professor, disgruntled with teaching Malays in his one composition course (he taught Technical Writing) had given the students an ESL exam and graded their essays according to their ESL score. What provoked an even greater anger in the students was the professor's refusal to use their names. He called them by an assigned number. Only six weeks remained in the term; and I was hired to save the day. Then weeks later I was offered a position as a full-time professor.

In decades of teaching, I had learned each student's name during the first day of class by using a simple technique. Each student told me an anecdote, and I hooked the story to a name and face. But in three classes each term in Malaysia, and no more than 60 students, I struggled to remember the names of female students who covered their heads with the traditional *tudung* or *hijab*. This meant I couldn't see the shape of a face or the style of hair. And in Malay culture the female countenance is supposed to remain expressionless. The names of the young men—whose hair, chins, length of foreheads, and expressive faces I could see, made it easy to remember their names.

When first hired, I was told that academic freedom as it existed on American campuses was supposed to be respected on the Shah Alam campus. Still, I was forewarned to keep discussion of Israel out of my classroom. I look back now at what I had no knowledge of then and feel some embarrassment; and I sincerely hope my words will not be misunderstood when I say it took teaching Malays to realize that stuffing does not necessarily flavor a turkey. My students were studying physics, chemistry, advanced mathematics, and computer science. The plan was for them to complete the required years at Indiana's Malaysian campus (one of several U.S. programs), then study in the United States until they completed a bachelor's and possibly a master's degree. This was stuffing.

At Indiana's graduation ceremonies, a ranking U.S. diplomat, fluent in Bahasa, would attend and provide a whispered translation of what the Islamic cleric (imam) was telling the students in his address. He repeatedly warned them to stay away from decadent Americans in the United States; and he reminded them of *Dar al-Islam* versus *Dar al-harbi*: of separate and incompatible worlds. If there was a Malay student (and I taught several hundred) who disagreed with his or her religious upbringing, I never heard a word of dissent the entire time I taught Malays. I did, however, hear dissent from my Chinese and Indian students at Petaling Jaya Community College where I taught part-time.

The political joke in diplomatic circles was that Malaysia's affirmative action was unique, a program designed to support the two-third majority Malays and suppress the minority Chinese and Indian populations. Which meant the students I taught in Petaling Jaya did not have the advantage of affirmative action. And despite their high marks on the national examination, they had not been awarded scholarships from the government to study abroad. These students were trying to get to universities in the United States through their own means. Generally, they were a clever, funny, outspoken group — though no one dared to be too outspoken in Malaysia.

Why is that?

The answer requires a look at sedition, the law in Malaysia that I did not initially grasp. Begun in 1948 under British colonial rule, this Act bans any action, speech, or publication that shows contempt toward the government or royal sultans.

It was during my time of teaching in Malaysia that Ayatollah Khomeini issued his decree of death (fatwa) against Salman Rushdie for *The Satanic Verses*. Apparently, the ayatollah's actions deviated from standard Islamic legal practice. But my students refused to discuss the fatwa or consider Rushdie's right to freely express himself in literature. I tried to engage the students, arguing that the Pope had not asked Catholics to murder the author of *The Last Temptation of Christ,* a novel (and film) offensive to countless Christians. Silence in the classroom.

In my second year in country, there was an outbreak of hysteria among girls in factories and secondary schools. This form of hysteria is a psychological phenomenon endemic to Indonesia and Malaysia. As an exercise in writing a cause-effect essay, I asked the students to consider all possible reasons for the hysteria, with the idea of exploring the behavior as related to Malay culture. The students had to read press reports and articles in journals, then work in groups, and list the possible causal agents in order of importance. Without exception, my Chinese and Indian students listed clothing as among the first or second cause of hysteria. "In this excessive heat and humidity, if you had to wear a wool cap on your head, another layer on top of the cap, plus two layers of polyester fabric to your toes, and work or study without air-conditioning, wouldn't it be reasonable to go momentarily mad?" That was a typical, non-Muslim response from the PJ students.

Not one group of Malay students listed anything related to clothing, which I realize now would have been apostasy or blasphemy to have done so. I posted the Malay lists in my Indiana classroom and placed the lists from the Chinese-Indian students there, too. No Malay student in my composition classes commented on the clothing issue, either aloud or in writing. One male student did pose a question in the journal I required of students. "Don't our Malay girls look beautiful the way they are dressed?" I wrote back: "It must be wonderful to sit in non- air-conditioned classrooms in a polo shirt and comment on feminine apparel. Perhaps you better do some serious thinking before you move to the United States where you'll encounter professors who are feminists." I did add that my view like his was culturally conditioned and drew a smiley face beside my words.

It's important to clarify something. Of the five foreign countries where my husband and I lived, we loved Malaysia best of all, as did my daughters. Yet what appalled me about teaching there was the pallid prose I received from students whose right to question authority dried up early in life because of religious indoctrination. With my secular and liberal mindset, that's the way I saw it.

What are some of my memories of teaching there?

Fasting month was a difficult time for students. For weeks my male students sat in sleepy silence while the girls waved their notebooks more furiously than ever to cool their faces. No water allowed from sunrise to sunset. The food was another issue, as I saw it. "Explain something to me," I said one morning in a provocative way. "You get up to eat before sunrise and have a large breakfast. You eat again in the evening when the sun goes down, thus breaking the fast. Then you hustle over to the stalls around midnight and eat again. This means you have three meals. You just alter the time you eat them. Please explain to me how fasting gives your body a rest and honors the hungry of the world?" No response, *lah!*

Obviously, fasting isn't about anything logical. It's about obeying a religious dictate and beyond my secular ken. I remember poor Jones from Sarawak who couldn't find a place to eat, as the stalls were shuttered in daytime during fasting month. Spotted eating fruit and drinking water, Jones was detained by the religious police until he produced his identity card that proved he was a Christian from East Malaysia. When I recounted this story to my Petaling Jaya students, they laughed and said of my students in Shah Alam … no choice, *lah!*

One of my students, Rashid, had blown out his eyes during

fasting month when he was fifteen and over-zealous with firecrackers. He got around the campus with the aid of a cane. Each time he wandered down the third-floor corridor, tapping his walking stick against the balcony's metal railings, I felt a stab in my heart. Years earlier in Napa, California, a blind student named Carl and his blond Lab had taken my film course. When it came to recounting dialogue and explaining sound effects, Carl was brilliant; and thanks to a Seeing Eye dog, he navigated the campus with speed and confidence.

In Malaysia, because of my experience with Rashid, I wrote an essay that argued the unfairness of the country denying a Seeing Eye dog to a blind person. Dogs were not forbidden in Malaysia, though I knew many Muslims still believed that dogs represented ritual impurity; that if a dog touched a Muslim, that person was unclean and required cleansing before prayers. But this old injunction was controversial. So why, I argued in the essay, shouldn't guide dogs be available for use in Malaysia? A former student, a young man I particularly liked, asked to read a book of essays I was compiling. I see Bashir standing in the doorway to my office, wearing tiny, round glasses on his smiling face, the gold of the wire frames reflecting sunlight. In handing him my collected essays I forgot about religious blind alleys. Bashir returned my book through another student and never spoke to me again. I was the enemy and my criticism had gone in like a dagger.

What was my transgression the day I threw a party for my students in Technical Writing? This had been a small and wonderful class, in which we did not deal with sensitive social and political issues. These students had moved from passivity to playfulness and problem solving; and I wanted to reward their performance. Which is why I had asked our Chinese amah to make a cake, one with diplomas and other symbols for graduates. I took the cake and soft drinks to class but forgot napkins. I ran back to my office to get them. When I returned, the room had been re-arranged. Normally the students worked in groups of mixed gender. Now they were segregated. This was a party, not a class, and they were not allowed to sit together. Then I noticed a student was missing, a young woman who wore only black, including black gloves, who kept her headscarf over her face whenever she left the classroom so only her eyes were visible. One day she had asked me if a coat was needed in Minnesota in January, and something about Nor's innocence deeply touched me.

The day of the party I learned that Nor had left because she could not eat a cake prepared in my kitchen where pork might have been cooked. "Wait a minute," I said. "Today when I drove out here, I passed a huge truck loaded with pigs, all snorting in the air. I breathed in their molecules. You are breathing them right now. But Nor can't eat a cake from a kitchen where pork might have been cooked?" As I look back on that day, I do have to ask myself why the fourteen who stayed for the party didn't claim my attention more than the one who left. Why? Nor's blind obedience set me off.

Yet the truth is that I seldom raised a squawk from those roosting in my composition classes where I attempted through essays to discuss social and political ideas. I did ruffle the feathers of one young man who could not accept a piece we read by Colman McCarthy, a peace-activist-journalist in Washington, D.C. The article angered Abdul, who appeared in my office that same day. In the next class I offered a brief lecture on American individualism and McCarthy's assumptions: namely, the right to question authority. My lecture didn't satisfy Abdul. He returned to my office, and only after a third visit, did he reveal his concern. He had been a rebellious child. He questioned everything until his father taught him a "necessary" lesson. The father placed his young son in a bag of dirt and ants, suspended the bag from a hook, and left Abdul there until he recanted, promised to obey and never question either his father or the village imam. I never doubted the veracity of Abdul's story and shudder to think of it now.

As a teacher of expository writing, I faced an almost impossible task with Malay students, who had learned it was acceptable to claim authority without providing evidence. "Mr. Russell is wrong." That statement rings in my head and recalls the day a female student said these words. We were reading a short essay, "What is Philosophy?" by Bertrand Russell, to explore the 'definition' essay. Russell called philosophy a no-man's land between science and religion. I'd finished explaining the phrase 'no man's land' when Nurul's hand shot up. "Mr. Russell is wrong." "Why?" I asked. "Because nothing can be between something and Allah." That is where the discussion ended for Nurul, a bit of onion for the stuffing, easily pushed to the side of the plate.

Then there was Nasir, a real writer, the only one I taught on Indiana's campus in Malaysia. Nasir's father, a poultry butcher in a tiny village, wanted his son to be an engineer. But Nasir's gifts weren't in science and math. He was brilliant in languages, history, sociology, and psychology. His first essay in English 131 amazed me. Writing in English, a second language, he had 'voice'. Psychology fascinated Nasir, and the psychology professor became aware of his dilemma. It's as if two American professors began fighting for this young man's right to exercise free will.

One day Nasir came to my office and said I would never understand his village Malay culture which, he added ruefully, had not heard of the Enlightenment. He had to obey his father, regardless of what it meant for his dreams. Nonetheless, faithful to my cultural myopia, I asked Nasir to see *The Dead Poets' Society*, being shown that year in Malaysian theaters. Later Nasir wrote me a note and said he appreciated the movie; that it had made him feel less alone. But he wrote that I was putting him in a terrible bind, and the bind he was already in did not allow him to do anything. "If I struggle, I only tighten a cultural rope." His words haunt me still.

At one time Malaysia offered the promise of a tolerant multicultural society. But a resurgence of Muslim fundamentalism has created a country more polarized than in earlier decades. Shortly before we left the country in late 1990, I read a scholarly work that posited a familiar argument about future shock. In the face of rapid change, Malays had retreated to orthodoxy and separation from other cultures.

I know my Malay students saw me as an oddity, a bird without a nest, a strange woman who drove into campus in her left-hand driven car in a right-hand country. I would pass the tennis courts on the way to the teacher's parking lot, see some of my female students wearing sweat-pants and long shirts, heads and chests covered, trying to run around a tennis court in 90 degree heat and humidity. As someone who played a lot of tennis in Malaysia, I would shake my head in sadness. I recall the day the "Mr. Russell is wrong," student told me about her weekend of rock climbing. "What were you wearing?" I asked, somewhat impolitely. "This," Nurel said, sweeping her hand over her head covering and Malay *baju*. "But sweat-pants. Not a long skirt." I chuckled, unable to suppress the paradoxical image that came to me: of wanting to be an eagle and ascend heights, while clad in the garb of cultural restraint.

Recently, I watched an Academy Award Best Foreign film, *Separation*. An Iranian woman, dressed in black, makes a telephone call to a religious authority to seek permission to help the old man under her care. He has dementia, and he has soiled himself. It is the woman's first day of work, and her young daughter is with her because she cannot be alone with the elderly man. This devout Muslim woman wants the religious authority to provide an answer: *If she helps the man and possibly sees his genitals, will she risk eternal damnation?*

How, I ask, is it possible for a rational, secular Westerner to understand and accept the indoctrination that forms the basis of this woman's question? And what gives anyone hope for compromise and peace in the Middle East, when Iran and Hamas are intent on destroying Israel, and so many within Israel's borders are equally unyielding about the Palestinians? Meanwhile, Syria's heinous civil war continues. Meanwhile, ISIS screams for Sharia law, enacting horrendous terrorist attacks around the world.

So many memories of my Malay days have returned, as well as revisiting that classroom at Air University in Montgomery. But to pretend there is a conclusion to my words would be to speak falsely. I can only say that I do not accept that God and the divine are about separate seas, and this means to keep rowing against fundamentalist currents wherever they are. We must educate humans to yearn for wholeness and to have in our minds always — the shape of our shared planet.

Malay Days/Separation
Intercultural Essay, 1st Place, 2012
Judge: Tara L. Masih

One Face from the Shadow of Millions

To write about Chano makes me feel tongue-tied—the way he was in the beginning of our lessons. Yet I do not need to navigate currents of difficult idiomatic English. "Tongue tied?" he asked one afternoon, wanting to know the Spanish for this expression. *"Timido para hablar,"* I said.

Long ago I put away a photo of Chano and his wife, no longer able to see their faces each day: the pensive stare in Chano's, the sadness in Minerva's eyes. At the time the photo was taken, she was in Virginia on a six-month contract to pick crabs. Chano, working for a contractor in the Northern Neck, was saying good-bye to his wife—until he could return home to his Mexican family. I kept the photo on my desk for the past decade because it reminded me that the White House and Congress have shamefully skirted our sticky *immigration issue,* with its staggering statistic of eleven million or more undocumented persons in the United States.

All these years of no action …

As I write these words, a cold anger passes over me and brings language, unlike the mute sadness I felt when the call came that March in 2007 from the Mexico-Texas border, where Chano's sister and his wife were searching for him. Chano had left Virginia in late December of 2006 and returned home to Mexico, disheartened that yet again immigration reform had stalled in Washington, D.C. And three months later he attempted his first (and **only**) illegal entry into the United States. It is important to note that Chano had paid federal and state taxes. He was studying English, too, and felt confident the expiration of his second work visa would be overlooked in an amnesty, which would mean he could continue working in Virginia and sending money home to support his family. Yet he knew, if he were caught entering the States illegally, that an arrest would destroy his dream.

The March day when Chano's sister Isidra called me, I could barely speak, even though I am conversant in Spanish. I could only tell her that my husband and his friend, a retired army major general, were doing everything they could to determine if Chano was being held in a detention center on the U.S. border. I reminded Isidra that her brother was a survivor and said she must not give up hope. Yet my words belied my feelings. When I hung up the phone, an odd word came to me: Waco (*el hueco*), Venezuelan slang for the neglected holes in the streets of the capital, a word I heard often while living in Caracas from 1991 through 1995. Yet *el hueco* has dimensions; it's a hole with a bottom, unlike the feeling I had in my heart as I stood by the phone in the cottage where I'd taught English to Chano: twice-weekly lessons that he paid for by working on our property.

In his full-time position with a contractor, he had used the social security card he'd been issued when he first came to the United States under contract to a landscaping company in Northern Virginia: a company that had not fulfilled its promise of full weekly employment to the workers brought in legally. Later, after he completed the first contract, Chano returned home to Mexico, then again entered the USA legally. When the second company's promises of full employment were unmet, he sought work at a factory that manufactures wood molding for windows and doors. This company hired undocumented workers and those with expired visas. The management would not accept Chano's legitimate social security card and told him to go to Washington, D.C., where illegal documentation could be bought easily. Paid ten dollars an hour at the factory, Chano sought a second job at night in a popular U.S. steak house. Whether Chano used his legal or his illegal social security card at the restaurant is something I never asked him. Yet later, working in Virginia's Northern Neck for the contractor, Chano paid all required taxes, worked hard to learn English, and expected to be granted legal status under a new bill for guest workers. Throughout 2006 he waited and hoped, until the campaign for presidential nominees heated up and action on immigration cooled.

It was never Chano's intention to stay here permanently. He loved his country. He had a house in Mexico City, a house he spoke of with pride, a house built from his own labor. His wife, adolescent daughter, and two sons lived there. His elder son was completing medical school; and the expenses for books and materials were the main reason that Chano initially sought work in the United States. For a decade, his sister and her family had been coming to Virginia to work in the crab industry, working half a year here, then returning to Mexico. Chano had not been home for three years, and his daughter missed him terribly. He told me it was essential that he be in Mexico for the celebration of her important 15th birthday, despite the difficulty that this presented. He could leave the USA with an expired visa but could not return.

Harsh weather during January and February meant the contractor did little work: a perfect time for Chano to leave, except for the problem of getting back. Another reason compelled him to return home, which involved his second son, rudderless after secondary school, especially after he failed to pass the exams to be a military officer. In December 2006, Chano told me he was returning home to put his house in order: *"para poner la casa en orden."* His decision meant, that if he returned to the United States, it would have to be an illegal entry with the expensive help of a *coyote.*

Before Chano left for Mexico just before Christmas of 2006, he came for dinner and told my husband that he would be driving his used Honda SUV home and had hired a company that "greased" the importation of older cars to Mexico. Throughout dinner that evening, Chano spoke only English. After three tours in South America, my husband and I speak Spanish, so Chano could have conversed with us in his language. But instead, and with pride, he spoke only English that evening.

In the beginning of our lessons, I asked Chano to memorize conversations, ones I wrote for him, plus long lists of vocabulary. From personal experience I knew the formidable wall that adults must penetrate to learn a second language. Yet before two years had passed, Chano and I were reading stories from *The New Yorker.* The last story we read was T.C. Boyle's, *"Sin Dolor"* (No Pain), a fictional narrative that involves the exploitation of a Mexican boy, whose genetic mutation means he feels no pain. No *physical* pain that is; and the boy get turned into a freak for a traveling show and put on display to demonstrate the inhuman pain he tolerates. Why had I chosen the story? The setting was familiar to Chano, and the prose brilliant. But I had not considered how the theme might affect him, and how it might offer words for his experience in our country. T.C. Boyle's story and the two that Chano and I read by the Peruvian and American writer Daniel Alarcón, address enslavement and exploitation.

After Chano left for Mexico, a story was recounted to me of the conversation he had with a widow, a woman he worked for regularly on weekends. She spoke no Spanish, so Chano that December of 2006, had sat in her house and carried on a long conversation in English. He told her that U.S. employers had made promises that were unmet. His current employer wanted him to remain permanently in the United States to work for him. But only with this agreement would the contractor begin the lengthy process of trying to obtain a visa through the Department of Labor. The contractor had no children, no real knowledge of Mexican culture, and apparently did not understand that he was asking Chano to abandon both his family and his country. When the conversation with the widow was recounted to me, I remembered the afternoon during a lesson when Chano had described an incident that occurred that same day, when a worker on a building site hollered at the contractor, "Hey, where's your slave?"

Slave ... *esclavo* in Spanish.

Did others of us enslave Chano? Had desperation made us throw out ropes and entangle him in our needs? As I write these words, I look around my study. Every book in my library is one from boxes that Chano carried into our new house the summer of 2006. He hauled hundreds of boxes from the garage, as well as the furniture he could carry by himself. At the time my husband was working in Afghanistan; and all during the time that Mike was away, I relied on Chano's help. One problem I faced was our house under construction. As part of the contract with our builder, my husband and I had agreed to stain all the interior pine trim, which meant when Mike left for Kabul in January of 2006, the task fell to me. Yet I was not alone. For hours on cold Sunday afternoons, Chano helped me stain the seemingly endless stacks

110

of four-inch wide, six-foot long, pieces of pine molding, like the ones he had made in the factory in Maryland. He worked quickly yet carefully, without any trace of my boredom and impatience. I might have put Chano's photo away, but I cannot avoid the seven trimmed windows in my study. I see him now, working over a wood horse that balanced the long pieces of pine, staining four to my one, our only warmth from a space heater, and outside the frozen fields of snow.

Every person in the Northern Neck who depended on Chano was counting on his return from Mexico. A friend gave me a key and left Chano's pay, assuming he would be back before her return from Florida. He could have filled his weekdays, not just his weekends, working for those who needed and appreciated his help. He never required supervision, only a list of what had to be done. Unfortunately, locals who do maintenance work are characterized as lazy and unreliable, whereas Chano was hardworking, dependable, and trustworthy. And Chano did not regard manual labor as beneath him, even though he had studied engineering for three years in a Mexican university before he married and had to work full-time to support a family. For fifteen years in Mexico City, he had worked in the printing business until the newspaper's most recent owner was implicated in drug trafficking, and the government shuttered the operation. Since schooling for Chano's three children was expensive, and salaries in Mexico were low, he took the opportunity to work in the USA. Then following his second legal entrance, he remained here. Undocumented does not describe the reality. Chano had documents. They were just out of date. Expired.

In late December of 2006 when I hugged Chano good-bye, I was too choked with emotion to speak. I am a person who seldom cries, and later that night my husband commented on the emotional farewell. I told Mike that I had felt I was saying good-bye forever and could only hope that my feeling of not seeing Chano again was because he would stay in Mexico. He knew the danger of trying to return to the United States, illegally.

Are those who needed Chano, who wanted him to return, who praised him excessively, not complicit in this injustice? As is our country, where molding for our homes might be made by scores of undocumented workers, where landscaping is done by Latinos under contract who might not be given the hours they were promised, where customers slice into thick steaks and don't see the workers out back in the shadows.

In the fall of 2006, before he bought his used Honda SUV, Chano drove a small sedan, and one night he collided with a deer, the car a total loss. The accident necessitated police reports and insurance claims. No one asked: "Are you a legal resident here?" He had sublet an apartment to fellow Mexicans in Maryland and when they left without giving the required notice, even though they had paid the rent in full, the landlord summoned Chano to court. In the courtroom he was not asked about his immigration status. And more than once he teased me that his Maryland driver's license had been issued for ten years and my more recent Virginia license was good for only three.

Que rio grande de hipocresia, no?

What a large river of hypocrisy, yes.

I will never know how bright the moon was that March night in 2007 when Chano returned to the Mexican side of the Rio Grande. *Chano's brother-in-law was the witness for what happened.* The large group reached the U.S. side safely—then was split. One group of men went ahead while Chano and three others stayed where they were on the U.S. side of the river. But word reached them that border agents were in the area and might have caught the first group. Chano knew if they, too, were caught, it would end his dream of obtaining legal status when the political wrangling finally stopped in Washington, D.C. That night he and the other three men did not stay on the U.S. side. They decided to re-cross the river, wait on the Mexican side, and make another attempt during the night. Yet in darkness who knows one part of the river from another? One of the men dropped into a deep hole and called out for help. Chano, already across the river, safely on the Mexican side, went back to help his *compadre*. That man's body was found the following day in the Rio Grande. Not Chano's.

For two years the river was a metaphor that he and I shared: a metaphor that speaks of plunging into the rushing currents of language, drowning in words, being swallowed by them, flailing against their opaque turbulence. I had seen Chano paddle, seen him sink in frustration, and watched how he boldly resurfaced. Page by page we worked our way through a pronunciation guide. One afternoon I proudly told him that his accent was far better than Mexico's President. He and I read Latino poets in translation, including collections by the Chilean poet, Pablo Neruda. I insisted that Chano rent *El Postino*, the lovely Italian film about a postman who discovers his voice through his friendship with Neruda. Chano's own day of linguistic triumph came when he argued with me in English, asserting his point of view, not acceding to mine because he lacked the words in English to be the intelligent man he was.

For two weeks that March of 2007, I kept repeating, "Chano's alive. He's a survivor."

Then during the early morning of March 31st, I dreamed that

Chano was in a hospital. It had been two weeks since I had spoken to his sister Isidra, and I knew that she, Minerva, and several friends were continuing their search along the Rio Grande. As soon as I awakened, I excitedly told my husband Mike about my dream. Taking me in his arms, he said the contractor had called with news on Sunday night when I was asleep.

Chano's body had been found at last ... in the black mouth of the Rio Grande.

After I heard the news, I stood outside the cottage where I write in the early hours and where I had taught English to Chano. And with bitterness, I asked myself if those who found Chano's body had thought ... *just another wetback*. This word no longer used has been replaced by *undocumented*, a convenient euphemism that hides the image of Latinos swimming a river to enter the United States. That morning, looking toward the departing moon, I recalled a favorite song of my youth, "Moon River" with its phrase ... my Huckleberry friend, and a river wider than a mile, and crossing it a dream.

As a teacher I have held the same belief that Franz Kafka voiced: "Literature should serve as the axe for the frozen sea within." Now, however, I wonder about my countless efforts to act on this belief. Was Chano served from reading, *"Sin Dolor?"* about the enslaved Mexican boy who felt no physical pain? Yet, in having

114

asked myself this question, I must reassert that I have found no better way to walk in another's shoes and to understand diverse cultural worlds than through reading good literature.

Following Chano's death, I sent a book of Pablo Neruda's poetry to his daughter, marking poems her father had liked. Yet the poet Chano appreciated more than Neruda was Roberto Juarroz from Argentina. A line from Juarroz haunts me now. *"Mi sombra me ha ensenado a adoptar otras sombras."*

My shadow has taught me to adopt other shadows.

Que verdad. How true.

After Chano there was Antonio. After Antonio was Manny. After Manny there is Carlos, as I will call him—since he is still here. He works in a cannery, pays taxes, learns English, works on his days off for some of those that Chano worked for; and Carlos dreams of the day when he will not have to live in the shadows. His future dream is to return to Mexico with enough money to start a business. He's an enterprising young man, a quick study, and he had the *cojones* to tell one man that *el senor* was asking a lot and paying too little, considering he had the means to pay fairly for help and not to exploit undocumented workers. Still, even if others of us pay fairly, we are complicit in an injustice, as are all of those who hire undocumented workers.

With Chano's daughter or his wife, I would not have shared the Juarroz poem that particularly caught Chano's attention. The poem was number 10, in the 1958, *First Vertical Poetry*, translated by the poet W.S. Merwin. It could be the lament of anyone in exile from his or her country of birth, anyone separated from his or her family, any person who might feel alone, anyone whose faith in a protective god has been shaken or never existed. I read the poem now and wonder whether Chano felt a foreshadowing of his death, as I had that December night in 2006 when he and I said good-bye. The poem as translated, says:

I think that at this moment
maybe nobody in the universe is thinking about me,
I am the one who is thinking me,
and if I were to die now
nobody, not even I, would think me.
That may be why
when you think of someone
it is like saving them.

The final lines are ones I will not forget, as I will not forget Chano. There was no saving him — not with our past and current immigration imbroglio. And I try not to think about what might have gone through Chano's mind when he realized the current of the Rio Grande was stronger than his strength to withstand it.

Yet often these days I think about the haunting first line of Robert Frost's poem, "Mending Wall." *Something there is that does not love a wall.*

One Face from the Shadow of Millions
Tara L. Masih Intercultural Essay, 2nd Place, 2013
Journalism Award: NLAPW Biennial/Letters,
1st Place, 2020

A Woman Reader from the Boogie-Woogie West

T*he Woman Reader,* written by Belinda Jack, a fellow at Christ Church/Oxford, documents the history of women and reading. In the book's final pages, the author describes the Sewing Circle of Herat, Afghanistan, where sewing served as the cover for women reading serious Western literature. Under Taliban rule, these women took a tremendous risk—because had they been caught, they could have been imprisoned, tortured, or even killed. The author's mention of this sewing circle, plus her long discussion of *Reading Lolita in Tehran*, provoked recollections of my experiences in three book clubs of women.

The first was in Alabama in 1979, where, as a native Californian I found myself in another country. Before moving to the South that year, I had been in a feminist 'consciousness-raising' (FCR) group in California's Napa Valley, where two female psychologists taught a group of women to be assertive. In the fall of 1979, I quickly realized the West Coast's FCR movement had not reached Alabama's capital. It's not important how I ended up briefly in a book club there. The woman who invited me to the meeting said to read May Sarton's *Journal of a Solitude,* which I'd read in California; and the choice of this memoir made me think I would be meeting women who embraced diversity.

That October evening in a lovely home (think *Southern Living*) no one mentioned Sarton's sexuality. I sat there, recalling a

Bloomsbury moment when Virginia Woolf's sister, Vanessa Bell, said "sex"—the first time anyone in that famous group of English intellectuals spoke the word aloud. I don't know if Vanessa belted the word or modulated her voice. But I asked quietly if anyone had read Sarton's novel, *Mrs. Stevens Hears the Mermaids Singing.* My question brought no nodding heads or waving hands. My feminist training told me to be more direct. "Sarton prefers mermaids." Blank stares told me I was still being too indirect. That's when I used the L word. Dead silence as the cliché goes. Obviously, I did not relate this story to feminist friends in the Napa Valley.

The club's next selection was Flannery O'Connor's *Habit of Being,* over five hundred pages of her letters published that fall of 1979. For a decade in the Napa Valley, a friend and fellow English teacher named Barry had been telling me to read O'Connor. I bought the expensive hardcover book, planning later to send him the *Habit of Being.* I read every page slowly, knowing that Barry would appreciate what I underlined and wrote in the margins.

In early November I went to the evening book club in another *Southern Living* home, more excited about a writer than I'd been since college, when I first read Franz Kafka's *The Metamorphosis.* The week before the book club met, I'd bought and read O'Connor's two short story collections: *A Good Man is Hard to Find,* and *Everything That Rises Must Converge.* The night the book club met, my exuberance for Flannery reached truly assertive heights. And because I was the only book club member who had read *Habit of Being* from beginning to end, I did most of the talking. Something other than not being a demure Southern lady set me apart in the book club. I was married to a practicing Catholic and, even though I was not one, this identity made me an outsider in a room of confirmed Protestants, who kept asking in multiple ways: How can anyone be Catholic? So, whose keen idea was it to read the Catholic O'Connor?

That evening I became a veritable dervish, whirled away by O'Connor's genius, seized by her letters the way Barry had hoped Flannery's stories would consume me, which now they had. The silence that entered the room during the first book club when I'd said *lesbian* was different in the second gathering. The fifteen or more members adjourned early to a table laden with desserts and chatted away, ignoring me. Who were they? Society ladies who wanted to augment social resumes with *book club associate*? Over coffee and cakes, no one mentioned the next book or where the club would meet in December.

Yes, indeed! Instead of literary *convergence*, this club of Southern ladies had black book balled its new member from California. No matter. My husband's posting to Air University in Montgomery was only ten months; and in that short time—because of this book club of Southern ladies, I'd found Flannery O'Connor, who became a transforming experience in my life. In the next two years in West Germany I wrote a master's thesis, with Flannery a large part of my M.A. work.

Although *dismembered* by the Alabama book club, eight years later in 1987, I joined a book club in Malaysia. This club was comprised of East Indian, Malay, Chinese, Canadian, and Australian women, who were Hindu, Muslim, Buddhist, and Christian. They invited me, a secular Californian, to join them. For three years in Kuala Lumpur, I relished this group of diverse women who read *only* novels of recognized literary value. We all agreed with Wendy Lesser, who wrote in *Why I Read*, that nothing takes you out of yourself the way a good book does, making immigrants of us, unbinding us from the comfort of one place and time, and offering exploration in wider cultural worlds.

Something else was special about this book club in Kuala

Lumpur. The members were educated, middle-class women, keenly aware of privilege, especially in a country where literacy had not always been the norm, especially for rural women. Each of us in the club had the privilege of live-in help in our houses, which meant we were largely free of domestic duties and had the luxury of ample time to read. And I, working as a full-time professor in Malaysia for Indiana University, could not have read what both my teaching and the book club required without a Chinese amah running our household. This privilege, which I and other book club members recognized, created a shared obligation to stretch our minds through the novels and philosophical works we read. We sought books that drew us into disconcerting conversations with 'self' and other members. Engagement was the word in this book club, not reading for distraction and escape. We met not to eat and chat but to discuss literature. This club was a genuine pleasure and, when I said good-bye in August of 1990, I felt deep sadness, sensing my experience in this group of women might be unique in my lifetime.

But fourteen years later, ten of them spent in three South American countries, it turned out that I was not finished with book clubs of Southern ladies. I fast forward to the Northern Neck of Virginia in January 2005. I am in an old friend's car. We've driven to the residence where the book club will meet. Vicki opened her door but hesitated before getting out. "I think you should know not everyone appreciated this book." She was referring to *Strapless*, a non-fiction work about John Singer Sargent's controversial portrait of Madame X. I had suggested this short book at the November meeting, only the second one I'd attended. Following our discussion that morning of *Love and Hate in Jamestown*, the club's organizer had asked if anyone knew of a short book for the January meeting. My mother in California had read *Strap-*

less a month earlier and liked learning about life in Paris, the advent of department stores, the art climate of the late 1800s, and the controversy over JSS's striking portrait of Virginia Gautreau (Madame X) in a black, strapless gown. *If Mom appreciated this book, these ladies will, too.* So, I opened the mouth I'd intended to keep closed, at least initially, in this new book club.

Outside an impressive brick colonial house that January 2005 morning, I asked my friend Vicki which members had disliked *Strapless.* She said her Episcopal priest's wife hadn't liked it, adding that I probably didn't know that one member of the book club had been a First Lady of Virginia, whose husband as governor had desegregated the state's public schools. Vicki had run into this former First Lady in town a few days earlier and heard, "I'm not sure I want to know *our* new book club member."

A week earlier in January, my husband Mike had left for tsunami-ravaged Banda Aceh, Indonesia, to work for the U.N. food program. This meant I was alone in the Northern Neck of Virginia and, except for Vicki, knew few persons. She had asked early in 2004 that a spot be saved for me in this newly organized book club. I'd arrived from Lima, Peru, in October of 2004, to "road's end" in rural Virginia by the Chesapeake Bay, fully intending to submerge my new age, consciousness risen California self and file down my 'tough as nails' persona from four years of helping incarcerated North Americans in Venezuela's infamous prisons. I envisioned in this place of retirement, not too distant from D.C. where our two daughters lived, a return to that time in the early 70s when outside of the classroom I was largely unobtrusive. Yet now a simple book, non-controversial in every way, had alienated me from women I'd either not met or whose names I hadn't learned.

Upon entering the house that January morning, I noticed the artwork—real art, with lights above fine oil paintings. *A perfect setting for a discussion of John Singer-Sargent.* With this thought, I stepped over to the fireplace and stood there alone, as if needing warmth, feeling unsettled about what Vicki had told me. Within minutes I was given a cool reception from the member who had led the discussion of *Love and Hate in Jamestown* at the November meeting. She set her purse down in a chair near me and offered no greeting. Odd behavior for a Southern lady, I thought. Glancing down, away from her unsmiling face, I saw the book she held. Thin like *Strapless* but with an off-white cover and what appeared to be a decapitated mannequin wearing a black bra in a barren landscape.

Trying to be friendly, I asked what she was reading.

"The novel you recommended."

"No!" I said, holding up the non-fiction *Strapless* with its striking black cover and the portrait of Madame X.

Oh, *merde!* I'd forgotten that book titles aren't copyrighted.

At the November meeting I hadn't remembered the author's name; and the book club's leader sent out an e-mail reminder to read *Strapless* for the January meeting. And several of the Southern ladies had indeed ordered *Strapless*, the first ever novel by a female American writer in which a young American named Darcy Baxter (not Henry's *Daisy Miller*) goes off to Australia to open a lingerie shop and has a passionate affair with a sheep farmer. Apparently, this novel from the Romance Alley genre is exclusively about sex. That winter's day I tried, teacher that I am, to lead a discussion on the *Strapless* that some of the ladies had read and some hadn't, all the while aware of the irony played out on me. I'd suggested a simple and innocent book without knowing that *Strapless* had a debauched twin featured on the Harlequin web site.

Seated close to the fire that morning, I recalled the Montgomery book club and a quote from May Sarton: "We have to dare to be ourselves, however frightening or strange that may be." So that late January morning before the book club adjourned for lunch, I took May's advice. I asked the Southern ladies to indulge me in hearing a personal story, one I thought related to the *Strapless* mishap. I told about the time in 1998 when my daughter Michelle, an army lieutenant living in Germany and recently engaged, had called me in Falls Church, Virginia, and asked if I'd seen any good movies lately. I knew Michelle could rent recent films through the army exchange.

Boogie Nights, I said. Good actors, smart director, interesting film.

The phone rang a few nights later in the early morning hours. My husband Mike was living and working in crazy Bogota, handling aviation for the State Department and the U.S. 'war on drugs'. I thought the worst might have happened. But it was daughter Michelle on the phone.

What the hell were you thinking, Mom?

About what?

That movie *Boogie Nights*. You might have said it was porn. Dirk Diggler and his big dick.

It was the middle of the night, or more accurately the early morning, and I wasn't up to arguing that *Boogie Nights* was an art film about the porn industry in L.A.'s San Fernando Valley. Who knew this U.S. sub-culture was so organized and widespread? But Michelle wasn't interested in what I thought. She and her fiancé, Patrick, had invited two couples over for a dinner party. That news woke me up.

You showed *Boogie Nights* to guests?

Yeah, Mom, and one guy wanted to know who'd recommended the movie. I told him, my mother. You know what he said? *I'd like to meet your mother.*

123

I laughed that night on the phone. Not daughter Michelle. And most of the Southern ladies didn't laugh either. A good way for a story to fall flat is to mention a movie that few have seen or dare to mention having seen. The nervous laughter from some of the bookies might have meant these ladies now classified me in the category that surfaces when we read a complex, demanding novel from a *master builder*. The mantra of this book club of Southern ladies is ... *the characters aren't normal*. Are the conventional, habitual, traditional, popular, average, middling and well-adjusted the norm in real literature, which offers peripheral vision into worlds unlike our own? And because I love masterful literature and hate what's shoddy and sentimental, I'm vociferous about what the British writer Fay Weldon calls Pre-Fab fiction.

In Weldon's short novel, *Letters to Alice,* she creates "the City of Invention" where *only* master builders get the heights. Below are the Pre-Fabs and districts like Romance Alley, which lead downward to that darkened alley where Porn resides. Weldon says the master builders, those like Jane Austen, carry a vision out of the real world and transport it into the City of Invention, enlightening the reader so that on her return to reality, that reality is changed, even if minutely. That is a gentle way to say what Franz Kafka said in fewer words. He claimed literature should serve as an axe for the frozen sea within us — a literary experience of turbulent waves and rough sand on unfamiliar shores — the human heart melted and yet enlarged. I thank Kafka for Gregor Samsa and *The Metamorphosis*. But in saying this I am admitting to my first rub related to literature: I haven't shed an illusion that art can effect change and offer a means toward moral refinement through its expanded visions of life.

The British philosopher and literary critic, Terry Eagleton, in a recent article, "The Hubris of Culture," states that "nobody believes any longer that art can fill the shoes of the Almighty." Not fill the shoes I would agree. Yet in the beginning *was* the Word. How could I have taught literature from 1966 until now, if I hadn't believed there was meaning in literature; that it is about more than "aesthetics orchestrated by language," a phrase I read the other day. How Flannery O'Connor would chortle at this dry academic claim.

My second rub is something identified by Belinda Jack in *The Woman Reader*. She states that, "Lone reading is an inherently, anti-social activity, and the onus on women has been and often remains, to be sociable and facilitate easy human relations — to be uncritical, not ranking, not discriminating, always warm-hearted." To hell with this behavior, I say, recalling what Flannery O'Connor wrote in a letter in *Habit of Being*. Right after her first novel, *Wise Blood,* was published and, at the insistence of her editor, the reticent O'Connor with her heavy Georgia accent attended a dinner party at writer Mary McCarthy's apartment in New York City. O'Connor said the guests regarded her as *a refugee from deep thought,* silent as she was, and not looking "intelligent enough to have written *Wise Blood*." The shy O'Connor contributed little to the conversation until Mary McCarthy began holding forth on literary symbolism, including religious symbols. Then O'Connor spoke fervently: "If the Eucharist is only a symbol, I say to hell with it."

Among the Southern ladies, I'm often a refugee of unwelcome thought. And a reader might wonder why malcontent me remains in this book club. One reason besides liking the women (as I call them) is the non-fiction we read. *The Hare with Amber Eyes* was a small miracle — a book I would have missed had it not been for this book club. Since 2004 there have been many non-fiction gems, which I would not have read on my own, focused as I am on reading literary fiction. Nonetheless, I admit to problems with the 'happy enders' as Flannery O'Connor called them.

In the book club, I enjoy playing the role of sheep dog, trying to keep the Southern ladies from straying off the mountain and munching grass in front of Pre-Fabs, which they've read about on best seller lists or in cheesy reviews on the internet. Ladies, I assert loudly, we are aging women. We do not have all the time in the world to read excellent novels, so why waste time on drivel? The California, FCR teacher in me must speak, reminding the ladies that if we read enough of the master builders, old and new, good literature will both entertain and inspire us. Please ladies, I assert … let us not sink into the bog of books written for desperate agents in an industry owned by huge corporate interests, which exploit the fact that book clubs of women and ladies comprise a large percentage of the market for novels these days. The New York moguls know that even if the industry's female readers are not necessarily assertive actors in life, they do not want passive female characters in the novels they buy. Don't you see, ladies? That is why both French sisters in that novel we recently read had to be heroic fighters against their Nazi occupiers. This Pre-Fab, written by a New York lawyer turned novelist, left my jaw hurting from the effort of grinding through the prose, not to mention having to process the glut of bloodless extractions from the internet, sans lived and deeply felt experience.

Frankly, I pass on rot.

Wait a minute, I say, staring at the phrase I've just written, which can be read in two ways. I hope to God (in the beginning was the Word) I am not passing on rot. But I do pass on most popular fiction best sellers—the kind intended to be swallowed quickly and forgotten, novels that cause no shudder in the mirror of self and world, novels in contrast to Marilynne Robinson's *Gilead* trilogy and her

126

brilliant early novel, *Housekeeping*. Since 2005 I've foisted all four novels on the book club, with *Lila* our selection one December. A few members even took the course I offered on Robinson that spring through the local community college.

I do recognize, however, that when it comes to literature, I suffer from projection, as the psychologists use the term—in my assertion that the Southern ladies, many of whom read primarily for escape, ought to read good literary fiction. I'm also aware that bookies who have staked their claim to preferring what's normal, probably do not identify with the Irish writer, Edna O'Brien, who said she would be much lonelier on earth without literature and might even have gone mad without it. I identify with Edna's words.

As daily light lessens, I remember the girl who believed she had time to read every noteworthy novel in the Fullerton, California, Public Library. Later I was that lost student at the University of Southern California who never had time to read a novel more than once for her literature classes, so she went to the lower level of Doheny Library and roamed the stacks, borrowing ideas from the academics about *Portrait of an Artist* and *Portrait of a Lady,* never trusting her own limited experience and the scant hours she could give to each novel.

Projection or not, I will stick to my assertion that a woman (or man) isn't a real reader of literature without a discerning, discriminating mind and heart; and that any novel worth reading must be read carefully more than once, if not several times. Obtrusively, I beat this drum in the book club of *Southern* ladies. An ever-expanding library of good literature, preferably in old hardcover copies, is my act of faith in literacy, which throughout recorded history women have had to fight for, as have those men who were and are enslaved by racism and poverty. I now carry in my mind the image of the women in Herat, hiding books beneath their sewing, willing to endure real danger in order to read good literature.

The late John Updike, whose love of language was so intense and compelling, said his form of prayer was to underline novels and make notes in the margins. This is what I learned from my deceased Catholic friend Barry, who is ever with me when I open a book and find his comments.

From my experience the ideal book club is one in which members dare to speak their minds, seeking through the imagination to unite with beings unlike themselves, striving to become intelligent readers who know in their hearts that complex fictional characters, like real persons, must be read closely and understood for what they are—a mystery. This in no way discounts Southern manners, as Flannery O'Connor reminds us in her brilliant non-fiction work, *Mystery and Manners*. As a writer, I take counsel from Flannery, who advised that a writer needs both humility and arrogance.

However, to end this essay, I'll ignore O'Connor's advice to writers and offer a cheeky claim from a well-traveled woman reader, which is simply this: The Southern ladies are damn lucky to have in their book club, one member from the *boogie-woogie* West.

A Woman Reader from the West
L. Miao Lovett Intercultural Essay, 1st Place, 2016
Grace Wofford Essay Award, NLAPW Biennial/ Letters
2nd Place, 2020

Three Artists in Arrested Time:
Tiempo Detenido

One day in 2016, a friend handed me *The New Yorker's* January 4th issue, already open to page 78, and "Divas Under Fire." "You'll appreciate this," she said with a sly smile. From reading the article, I learned the opera version of Ann Patchett's *Bel Canto* had opened in Chicago. In his review of it, the music critic Alec Ross wrote: "The opera, like the novel, inhabits a world of make-believe, in which the magical power of music melts the hearts of terrorists and fosters bonds of affection, even of love." Ross went on to state the novel's "central conceit of a celestial voice that soothes savage beasts is a feeble one, and Patchett's vague musical descriptions fail to flesh it out. Moreover, the conceit is difficult to translate into opera." Ross asked how it was possible to perceive the transforming power of one voice with everyone singing?

I thanked my friend for the magazine, as it encouraged me to re-open a file marked *Tiempo Detenido*, that begins with these words: "On December 17, 1996, the *Túpac Amaru* Revolutionary Movement (MRTA) seized the Japanese ambassador's residence in Lima, Peru. Half of the five hundred guests at the national day celebration were quickly released. A second group of hostages left days later. And 72 captives were held until April 22, 1997. One hostage released before Christmas was a well-known Peruvian artist of Japanese ancestry, Carlos Runcie Tanaka."

From 2002 through 2004, I lived in Peru, and Carlos became my friend, as did Vera, a photographer who documented Peru's armed conflict between the government and revolutionary groups like the MRTA and *Sendero Luminoso*. In 2004 I had agreed to edit Vera's book, a photographic account of the decades of violence she had witnessed. A third artist with a connection to Carlos and Vera is Ann Patchett, who fictionalized the 'real' hostage story in *Bel Canto*. After reading *The New Yorker* review, I searched my files for a folder with Vera's name, found narratives I had written, e-mail we exchanged, and much more. That same day I looked for *Bel Canto* in my library, having decided to explore the intersection of three artists, to see what I might discover about their arrested time, their *tiempo detenido*, and mine as well.

Carlos: *Lluvia de Oro* (*Golden Rain*)

On this winter's day in Virginia, my thoughts take me to Peru where a summer sun has returned to Lima. Before moving there in 2002, nothing prepared me for the capital's relentless gray skies and the thick cloud cover (*garúa*) that prevails for months.

The first time my husband and I visited Carlos's home, we saw clusters of flaming orange flowers, *lluvia de oro*, spilling from the outer walls of his residence. Carlos calls the wildly growing evergreen vine "golden rain;" and like a refiner's fire, the flower's flaming color announces the dweller inside: a potter, sculptor, and installation artist. *El Museo de Carlito*, as I came to call his house, is the permanent exhibition of one artist's territory, which stores the installations he has given the art world since 1977.

When I first met Carlos, a line from William Blake came to me: "Energy is eternal delight." Yet within the nervous confines of a post 9-11 world, what happened to the energetic Carlos in a U.S. airport? Early in 2002, returning to Peru from Alfred University in New York where he had been the Visiting Professor of Ceramics, he faced a long delay in Miami. To pass the time until his flight to Lima, he began making his origami crabs. In folding paper, Carlos says he folds memory and time. That day in Miami he made tiny versions of his crab, kept moving around the airport, leaving a crab behind on an empty seat, like an offering. What alerted airport security? Was it Carlos's shaved head and distinct facial features of East and West? Or his tiny white origami crabs? Security officials escorted Carlos to a small room and questioned him—this artist who, ironically, had been a MRTA hostage six years earlier.

Before I ever met Carlos, I had seen one of his installations during the U.S. Embassy's annual *Night of Art* at the ambassador's residence. The festival's organizers had given him the area of the swimming pool. And he had used the black lines at the bottom: three rows, 3 x 12 = 36, his Japanese grandfather's age when he drowned in the sea at Ancon (Peru) in 1940, the same age (36) when Carlos almost drowned in Pasamayo, 100 kilometers north of Lima. For the installation Carlos strung three wire cables from end to end, following the pool's black lines. From each cable he suspended 12 plastic/acetate digital photographs, which resulted in 36 large, submerged images of a blue crab, and the face of his grandfather, Guillermo Shinichi.

That evening when I looked at the pool, I had no idea what I was seeing. With so many guests milling around, I couldn't get close to the words on a nearby wall that explained the 36 exposure/film processing pool as an attempt to merge the lives of two men, oriental and occidental, who met through their grandson's imagination. Walter Osbourne Runcie Stockhausen was a pioneer in aviation and aerial photography; and Carlos never forgot his grandfather's film-processing tanks, and the negatives hung on a line to dry. Yet it was through his Japanese grandfather, a man he never knew, that Carlos discovered his crab cosmology. The crab, though literal, is a metaphor: something real yet mythical, making a deceased relative into a living presence that travels on the artist's back, like the warrior crab in an old Japanese tale.

Carlos tells the story of surfing in Pasamayo, some ten kilometers from Ancon where his grandfather died—of a huge wave churning him to shore, of coming to consciousness there, and realizing that like his grandfather, he might have drowned. Then all around him, the eyes of crabs. This experience, however, required another to reach symbolic importance. At *Cerro Azul in Canete*, 130 kilometers south of Lima, while enjoying a picnic with his family, Carlos spotted crabs near the monument that commemorates the arrival of Japanese immigrants to Peru in 1899. Near the obelisk, he found thousands of dried crabs "silent in the sand," and began gathering them.

The crab is Carlos's alter-ego: moving quickly, digging holes, searching for water and shelter, leaving tiny balls or spheres on the shore, then resting to generate new energy. In the hands of this Peruvian potter, a symbolic creature emerges from a flat piece of paper. Yet without knowing the artist's personal history, it is understandable why Carlos and his repetitive folding of paper alerted 'security' in the Miami airport.

The crabs are everywhere: symbolic ones atop ceramic spheres, desiccated ones in glass boxes, crab images in historic Peruvian pottery, and crabs that friends find and give to Carlos. One day he and I found an ivory crab in an antique shop near the U.S. Embassy. Carlos paid almost the asking price. He had to have the crab, admitting his attraction to objects that provide clues to what we seek in life. This relates to another of his beliefs—about crowding every moment with things of beauty. Quoting a Japanese master potter, Carlos believes the "Kingdom of Beauty" is nowhere if beauty abides in only a few artifacts created by a few artistic geniuses. He carried this idea away from Japan, after apprenticeships there: beauty as ever-lasting awareness. "Japanese masters work hard throughout their lives to attain perfection," Carlos told me, adding that he had learned enough from masters to keep doing sound work but lacked the time to experiment with new glazes, clay, and firings. He would like to do "those smooth, white, clear surfaces," but has stayed with Peru's rough landscape.

In Carlos's studio I observed a meeting of East and West, where instead of the traditional *saki* as an offering to Kami Sami (the god of fire), wine or *pisco* is offered. The universal substance of salt, *la sal de la tierra*, is always set before the kiln. The fire is where objects must suffer an intense process, one in which the potter places his or her faith. When Carlos says, "Tomorrow I fire the kiln," the words are spoken with reverence. In the room where he keeps the objects he sells, he enacts another ritual by carefully wrapping his creations in heavy brown paper, then binding them with *mimbre* (raffia) and attaching his trademark card, which bears a circle. He calls this ritual "clothing the spirit of things, in order to reopen them." His generosity like his energy is apparent, as if the need to amass things must be balanced with his need to give them away.

In the year I visited Carlos's territory, I regained energy from wandering around his house, garden, and workshop: touching ceramic objects, seeing everywhere colors of land and sea: the red of clay and earth, the orange of flame flowers, and cobalt blue like a hidden jewel. In his garden, wherever I looked, were circles, recurring like Carlos's spheres. And everywhere veins of repair: broken pieces put back together, the fragments forming a different object, carrying the old spirit into something new. The scars from joined fragments spoke of time and fire and passion; of an artist always creating new forms.

From observing him at work, I began to understand clay as a humble substance, of the amorphous given shape; that the potter is ever respectful of the secrets and distances that clay must travel: a substance carried by wind and water, again turned to rock, thus repeating nature's process, the wheel going round and round, the carousel of time, *a circle game in which we look behind from where we came.* And like song writer Joni Mitchell, Carlos wanted to be a singer. While studying in Florence and Milan, his art instruction taking place within the museums and architectural wonders of those Italian cities, the "struggling artist" played his guitar in the streets for pocket money.

Prescience: The Intimation of Something to Come

In 1996, clay figures suddenly appeared. Carlos recognized them as his need to put together his head (philosophy) and his hands (ceramics). He press-molded the figures but modeled the hands. This made each figure unique.

When Carlos and 224 hostages were released before Christmas from the Japanese ambassador's residence, he returned home. In his workshop the clay figures were there, waiting. More than one hundred, ready for their first firing. Carlos's installation *La Espera* (The Waiting) was shown at the 1997 International Fair of Contemporary Art in Madrid, Spain. Experience and art had come together in a mysterious way, Carlos told me. "Figures, resigned in their overcrowding, subjected to another's will, yet masters of something inalienable — of self."

And the mystery known as *prescience?* Just hours before Carlos's release that December of 1996, he caught a glimpse of a bird in a tree, calm and quiet in the Japanese ambassador's garden. In life's circle game, the image of this bird spun Carlos to the terrace of his home, a place where strange experiments and actions often occurred. He recalled a day in late summer 1996, months before he was a hostage: "A fine morning dew, the garden wet. Suddenly, I heard a strong sound against the window. I thought it had broken. But a dove walked away. When I looked at the glass … such an impressive sight! The dove was wet, so the dirt and rain on her body left an imprint. I called my mother, who is always a good witness to these events. I asked if she had red lipstick. With it I drew a circle on the glass around the dove's silhouette and wrote, *Tiempo Detenido*."

Arrested Time, Time Standing Still, Time Lingering

In April 1997, government forces penetrated the Japanese ambassador's residence, killed the fourteen MRTA, and freed the 72 hostages. After this event, Carlos created his next installation, *Tiempo Detenido*, for Lima's first *Bienal Iberoamerica* in October 1997. Visitors passed through corridors to a room divided into four sections; and within the sections were 250 ceramic figures, 200 lights, 30,000 pieces of red crystal. These objects created an oppressive environment, as did raised hands that made shadows on the walls, with tiny lights flickering inside metal and glass rectangular low-lying boxes. The figures varied: some decorated with circles, others non-descript in earthen clay. Yet all were distinct because of their hands.

Then, like a metaphorical crab, Carlos moved on.

On the last day I visited him in September 2004, he was flying around, getting ready to leave for Brazil and his latest installation. He and I stood on the terrace, watching his assistant pour two thousand clear marbles into a large turquoise sphere. Three blue clay figures surrounded the sphere, as if reaching out to it. "Helpless," Carlos said, " yet still trying in a world deformed by circumstances. Or a world hit badly by circumstances." Struck by Carlos's words, I wrote them down.

A World Hit Badly by Circumstances

How strange to recall his words a few months later when the tsunami occurred, and my husband rushed off to join a U.N. team in Indonesia. Something else strikes me from that day with Carlos. I mentioned Ann Patchett's *Bel Canto* and said reviews described the novel as a romance about the 1996 MRTA hostage crisis.

"A romance?" Carlos said, drawing back, a perplexed look on his face. "It cannot be. You do not want to think about the toilets after one week." Then as always, his energetic delight sparked, and Carlos laughed, which brought my laughter, too.

Vera: Blood Like Rivers,
the World is a Microcosm (Leonardo da Vinci)

The forecast Nor'easter did not bury us; and this morning when I opened the backdoor, I saw only a dusting of snow. On a wall beside the door is one of Vera's brilliant images, which she enlarged and gave me on the day I left Lima in September 2004. Two years later, after our house in Virginia had been built, I placed the 24- by 15-inch photograph where I would see it each time I opened or closed the door—as a reminder of privilege.

The image is of a lone indigenous woman, tiny in body, old in years, clad in a red cape, crossing a narrow road in an Andean village. It has rained heavily, and thick mud is under her feet. Near the woman, a dog forms the other side of a triangle of three figures. The dog's back, covered in mud, is curved like the back of this elderly Andean woman. The dog's facial features, like the woman's, are hidden. At the apex of the triangle is a man leading a horse in the direction of a mountain. Except for his hat at the side of the horse's head, the man is invisible. The imposing mountain in the background appears only as a solid line in the gray sky. On both sides of the road, the doorways of houses appear as dark rectangles, and mud covers the lower half of once white-washed walls. Above the walls are mud-colored tile roofs. Yet there in the middle of the road is the woman; and covering her head and falling below her knees is a vibrant red cape.

In thinking about artists and remembering the years in Lima, I see why Carlos's art, home, and garden held such meaning in 2002. In Bogotá, where my husband and I lived for three years before Lima, we enjoyed a large apartment in a five-story building on a quiet street with a nearby park; and the 8000 feet elevation meant cool air and frequent rain. The move to sea-level Lima had been sudden and unwelcome: a 12-story apartment building on a busy street, the capital's pollution rivaling Mexico City, and no rain to wash away Lima's foul air. The apartment had wall-to-wall, floor-to-ceiling mirrors. Wherever I turned, I saw an aging woman. The living-dining room windows extended across the front of the apartment and provided a view of the country club across the street, and tall buildings in the distance.

We arrived in Peru during the hemisphere's summer. I quickly developed dry eyes and could not use contacts. An ophthalmologist said my eyes would be fine when I left polluted Lima. Then winter came and the *garúa* arrived. "A six-month frosted desolation," the sea-faring writer Herman Melville had written of Peru's capital and the strange, lingering fog. *Garúa,* an ugly-sounding Spanish word, suits this yearly fog that shows up like an unwanted guest and does not leave for months. Between the climate and the mirrored apartment, I disliked living in Lima's *San Isidro*, and envied embassy personnel whose apartments were by the ocean in *Miraflores*. The sea in Lima, if not always seen, could be heard there. Then out of nowhere, a cosmic gift: the energetic, artful Carlos. I only wish it had not taken until much later to meet Vera.

A friend of Vera's, a U.S. citizen and long-time resident of Lima, had heard I taught writing, and one day she called me. Married to a Peruvian, this woman cared deeply for Vera and worried that she was not going to act on an offer to send her book of photography to a major New York publishing company. What had stymied Vera was the editor's request for a narrative story to accompany the photographs, which the editor greatly admired. Vera spoke and wrote Spanish, German, and English. But the struggle to say in words what an image conveyed in an instant, emotionally and intellectually, left Vera unable to complete the book and send it to New York.

If Carlos's residence was a garden of earthly delights, Vera's crowded apartment was a jumble of things that contained her photo studio, her adolescent daughter's morass, her mother's remains of a photographic career, and Vera's own extensive archive from Peru's decades of violence. Vera struggled financially and, while waiting for AP assignments, shot portraits of the privileged (*los prilegios*) to support herself and her daughter.

In many ways Vera and I were kindred spirits. If family and friends thought I'd gone over the edge from 1991–94 in Caracas, Vera found my actions on behalf of incarcerated North Americans in Venezuelan prisons reasonable, even laudable; and she eagerly read my book, *Beyond the Wall*, published through a grant from a foundation in New Jersey. Yet nothing I had done in Venezuela seemed courageous compared to Vera's work as a photojournalist.

The rough surfaces that Carlos explored in his art were the terrain and landscape that Vera trekked to photograph the bloody conflict between *Sendero Luminoso* (Shining Path), MRTA, and Peru's counter-revolutionary forces. Carlos, protean like the clay he wedged to a wheel, had created installations from the violent event of December 1996, then moved on. Vera remained in *tiempo detenido*. I knew she could not pay for my editorial help, but I believed in her book and agreed to edit her prose, hoping to make her story as truthful and compelling as her brilliant images.

Early in the 1980s, Vera had begun traveling into the Andes where the indigenous did not welcome outsiders, especially women like the German-educated Vera, a mix of cultures, a woman with long, light-colored, untamed hair, penetrating eyes, and intense intelligence. She wanted to document the violence and to understand the evil of racism. How does abandonment, a fear so deeply imbedded in humans, leave people subject to indoctrination by revolutionaries like the Shining Path and MRTA? What Vera found was darker and more terrifying than she could have imagined. "I would have made a Faustian bargain," she told me one day, "and sold my soul to the devil … to get the images that screamed not to be forgotten."

Wandering into an Andean world she did not know meant that Vera had not taken the myth of the *pishtaco* seriously. This half-human, ruthlessly cruel Andean vampire is said to ambush travelers in dark and desolate places where only the whistling winds can be heard in the silence. By the time the traveler hears the footsteps, it is too late. The *pishtaco* decapitates the victim, extracts its fat, and the victim's body disappears without a trace. This myth, associated with the historic exploitation of the indigenous, takes different forms in Peru's history. The *pishtaco* of Ayacucho is white or *mestizo*, or a *gringo* with blue eyes. The myth of the *pishtaco* was important enough for the famous Peruvian writer, Mario Vargas Llosa, to have used it in his novel, *Death in the Andes.*

According to the myth, the first exploiters of the indigenous were the Spanish, who needed human fat (grease) to achieve extraordinary shine on their religious statues. From human fat they made candles for religious worship and used the grease to give church bells a sonorous ring. The extracted fat was also shipped to Spain to treat an unnamed disease; and later the fat of indigenous people greased the engines of English-owned railways in the central Andes. Much later in the 20th century, the fat and grease were exported to the USA for lubricating weapons of war and our space program. And current myth had it (as Vera traveled rugged Andean terrain) that then President Alan Garcia, thanks to the *pishtacos*, was paying Peru's foreign debt with human fat.

One day Vera asked the woman who cleaned her apartment if she believed in the existence of the *pishtaco*. The woman went into a long story about the *patrón* that her father had worked for prior to the agrarian reforms. She told Vera that the *patrón* had a room for extracting fat from his victims, that he liked to eat someone's liver on bread. "She told me this in such a matter-of-fact way that it all seemed possible," Vera said, "and I did not dare ask if she thought I was a *pishtaco*."

Listening to Vera made me feel once again that I was an ignorant American. In the early 1990s, before moving to Venezuela, I knew little about what was going on in the Andean region, except the War on Drugs. In 1990-91, my husband and I studied Spanish at the Foreign Service Institute outside Washington, D.C. One day the students who would be going to the Andean region were shown *La Boca del Lobo* (Mouth of the Wolf), a movie version of the November 1983 Socos massacre near *Ayachuco*, about which

I knew nothing. Then in 2004, I edited Vera's account of that same November 13th massacre, when *sinchis*, the civilian arm of the National Police, killed 32 villagers and blamed it on the Shining Path. From being in Socos and shooting film, Vera was threatened, only one of the many times she received death threats.

In *Yyanapag, Para Recordar*, the Truth and Reconciliation Commission's book from an exhibit in 2003–2004, there is a two-page centerfold with one of Vera's photographs taken as the 32 bodies were unearthed in a gorge by the river in Socos. Blood like rivers ran there—and in so many of the other places where Vera photographed the "orgies of violence" that both sides perpetrated. "I wanted to grasp it all, like some epic novel," she said one day, explaining that a history teacher in Germany had influenced her greatly. The horror had to be kept alive, documented for all to see:

What Had to be Eschewed Were Images
That Fed Escapist Illusions

If Andean peasants and other citizens found themselves trapped between revolutionaries and counter revolutionaries, Vera was there, too. From one side, she was thought to be producing propaganda for the *Sendero Luminoso* and MRTA. From the other view, it was claimed she worked for the government to undermine the revolution. Both sides saw Vera as their enemy and assumed she was making a pile of money from her photographs. And many of the indigenous saw Vera as a *pishtaco*. *"Gringa que haces aquí?"* she would hear said in a menacing tone. *What are you doing here?*

She was giving witness through images—and I never knew exactly how many she had. The problem was to choose from the countless images only a limited number to tell the story. How to create cohesion other than through time and place, which Vera rejected? Then one day in her apartment with hundreds of small prints scattered around, I picked out the lone Andean woman in her red cape and knew Vera had her thematic thread. She could use red. Carlos had used the color to create an oppressive environment for his installation, *Tiempo Detenido*. Red signified revolution, but the color held older, deeper meanings, such as the refiner's fire. Red also suggests anger, which Vera expressed after I broke my promise, the one I had made to her in Lima.

I can muster excuses for the winter of 2005: husband with the U.N. in Banda Aceh (Indonesia), one daughter in the U.K., our older daughter an Army company commander in North Carolina, her husband stationed in Bosnia, their three-year old daughter when ill unable to attend childcare, so my help was needed. Add to this being in the Northern Neck of Virginia, where I knew almost no one, living in a tiny cottage beside a garage, no builder for our house yet, everything stored in crates and boxes, including my library, dial-up internet the only option in the area, an electrical storm taking the surge control and computer one night, heavy snowfall that blocked our road the next. No sooner was my computer repaired than Vera sent pages of rambling text and this message: "My computer had over 180 viruses. I could not open e-mail …. I've come across some interesting connections between the *Inkarri* myth, the *Taki Onccoy*, the dance of sickness, dancers painted red …" I read these words and heard in my head a resounding no, violated a code of friendship I had tried to live by, and broke my promise to Vera.

Everything I have written is as true as memory can make it. Yet the words don't disclose my truth; that I was afraid to endure an intense process—the refiner's fire, fearful that I couldn't write the lucid, compelling narrative that Vera's brilliant images deserved; and afraid, given our physical distance, that she and I could not get to the heart of her complicated story. In the months before I

142

left Lima, seated beside Vera, she and I had begun to make sense of her story and get it down on paper. She had said then and written later in e-mail: "Please we cannot let go of this project." I did let go, rupturing a friendship I valued. Then worse than what I had done, I wrote a letter, as if words might mend my action. Again, the words I wrote were truthful; but I kept my timorous fears hidden.

Dear Vera ... Everything you need is in your apartment in Lima: boxes of testimony, piles of prints, drawers of slides. Your images are brilliant, as is your story of a photojournalist who wanted to understand the violence. Your photographic record takes the pain of an insane, obscene time and creates something from it. Your work gives voice to those who have no voice. Recently I came across an old article titled, "Kissinger Declassified," about U.S. complicity in the 1970s Chilean violence:

> The word *desaparecido* was the special new expression that was added to the bulging, lexicon of terror and dictatorship in the 1970s. In English it simply means 'the one who has disappeared.' But when pronounced in Spanish it possesses, at least to my ear, a much more plaintive and musical tone. As if you could hear the lost ones crying out, still. It has an awful lingering attractiveness to it, which becomes chilly and almost pornographic when you reflect how long and how loudly they were made to scream before they were dispatched, then buried like offal and garbage.

The article's author, Christopher Hitchens, could have been describing Angelica's testimony. This Andean mother's words cannot remain in a cardboard box, Vera. Who else in Peru besides you has so many of the testimonials? Will it be only scholars who are able to read rag-bone files in Peruvian archives? Now, re-reading some of Angelica's translated testimony, I hear her plaintive voice:

After 15 days, Arquimides sent me a note, saying: "Mamacita, I am here in the army base. Please urge them to let me go. Find money to pay a lawyer." We demanded, we urged, but my son never came out. From the base he disappeared. Until this day we do not know. We hear rumors that he is alive, over here or over there. That is why, to this day, I search for my son.

I will never forget Angelica's descriptions of finding bodies, the heads strewn like pumpkins in fields. These were images you captured through your lens. There was the day when Angelica went into a cave, calling out her son's name, going farther and farther into a hole she described as full of souls. She ended by saying: *"In my dreams, my son calls out to me. Mamacita, look for me next to the big rock where there is a straw hut. I am right beside it. The stream there is crystalline and clear."*

Crystalline and clear? What a contrast to the image of women and children above the gorge in Socos as the bodies of mutilated villagers were unearthed. I have not forgotten your description of their plaintive cries: *"From above the ridge, like a chorus in Greek tragedy, the voices of women and children filled the gorge with a mournful Ayatqui lament, a song for the dead: Why did you have to die this way? Why did you not remain in the house? What shall we do without you?"*

You, Vera, were willing to put aside your safety to document the atrocities in Socos. The last paragraph of what I edited haunts me. "Around three in the morning the phone rang, and a male voice said: *'El que sabe mucho ... muere in Ayacucho.'* (The one who knows too much, dies in *Ayacucho*.) With your love of justice, your respect for life, your belief in the need to document the truth, would you leave your book in that bloody riverbed in Socos? Will you not go on to tell the story of what happened before

144

and after that phone call when you were told you could die for having the courage to document the Socos massacre?

Eugene Smith, one of your heroes, described the shutter's release as "a shouted condemnation, hurled with hope that the picture might survive through the years, and at last echo through the minds of humans in the future." Your brilliant images resemble insects boring into the prickly pear that grows wild in Peru. From that incessant boring, a dark red dye is created: *Carmin Encendido*. Although red speaks of revolution in a modern sense, in so many of your images there is the older promise of red as alchemy, of base metal transmuted to gold. *Amiga mia* ... do not give up.

Vera severed communication.

Lo que queda? What remains?

On this winter's day, I have searched the internet and found an interview with her. The site says "private" and I was not able to open it. In a photograph, Vera looks exceptionally well, her long hair shorter. In another site I learned about the grant she received to print her photographs for the historical record they offer in Peru and elsewhere. I can only hope that like Carlos, Vera has moved on.

I have stopped writing to look at one of the most arresting photos in *Yuyanapag, Para Recordar,* the Truth and Reconciliation's exhibition of photographs from the decades of revolutionary violence. Vera's image is of a young couple wearing hoods and sitting on a cot. The black letters MRTA are above the holes in hoods that cover their eyes. The man holds an AK-47. The same gun is beside the woman because her lap has no place for a weapon. Seated, she holds a beautiful baby, a few months old. The infant girl gazes upward at her mother's face, hidden behind a red hood brighter than blood. The image made me think of Ann Patchett's *Bel Canto,* a novel that would illicit no laughter from

Vera about the MRTA's 1996 capture of the Japanese ambassador's residence in Lima.

What would Vera's reaction be to this novel? Disheartened outrage, I assume, given her deep belief that escapist illusions must be carefully and purposely eschewed.

Ann: Arrested Imagination

This morning a heavy mist obscures my view of the creek and surrounding marshland, and reminds me of Lima's seasonal fog, the *garúa*. For months from a fifth-floor apartment in *San Isidro*, I could not see the green fairways of an exclusive country club, the domain of Lima's privileged rich. Close by in *San Isidro* was the Japanese ambassador's residence where Carlos was held hostage. Whenever I walked to a nearby supermarket in the zone of *los ricos*, whether there was fog or not, I clearly saw the Indian mothers outside the market with babies in their arms. Their older children held small bags and sold wrapped candies, offering a few in exchange for money, as if to say ... *we are not begging*. On a nearby avenue, children regularly dashed into traffic with a rag and a bottle of water. The drivers usually wagged angry fingers at the children to keep them from cleaning their car windows before the lights changed. Alongside roadways I would pass Quechua-speaking mothers, waiting together while their children tried to wash windshields. The women seemed always to be parting the hair of their children, picking something (presumably lice) from the heads of those in their arms or laps.

These images were in my mind long before I saw Vera's disturbing photographs of Peru's long, internal, armed conflict. Through her stories, I began to understand why so many of the indigenous had fled their villages and come to the capital. The same had been true in Bogotá. After moving to Lima, I quickly realized

146

that traveling either north or south from the capital meant passing unimaginable slums, which depending on how far one drove, morphed from brick to thatch to cardboard. Although it disturbed me to live in a place where it almost never rained, I recognized the dry landscape in and around Lima as a blessing for those who lived in poverty. Years later the devastating floods in Lima showed what happens when excessive rain hits an area unprepared for it.

My impressions of Peru piled onto images already in my mind from Venezuela. There were the years in Colombia, too. In 2000, while living in Bogotá, I received a grant and wrote a book about Venezuela's prisons and the country's corrupt judicial system, which I experienced during four years of helping incarcerated North Americans there. Bogotá was something of a prison, too. To travel any real distance by car from the capital was considered dangerous; and the U.S. Embassy prohibited most travel because of the country's three terrorist organizations, the largest being the FARC. Each day my reading of Colombian newspapers brought troubling images. One horrific event, complete with photos of the woman involved, led to a recurring dream—of a collar bomb around my neck. A married couple, owners of a large hacienda, had refused to pay a monthly sum to the FARC, so a collar bomb with a timer was put around the woman's neck. The terrorists demanded a huge payment from the husband, which had to be paid before nightfall. The terrorists left and the couple called the police. Hours later the woman, and the two policemen trying to deactivate the bomb, were blown apart.

My brief revisiting of the past is to explain my reaction to Ann Patchett's romantic *Bel Canto* when I first read it, and later re-read it. Now, these many years later, the fog lifts before my eyes and, watching dark forms of trees emerge from the marshland, I recall a boy of eight in a Catholic orphanage in Caracas. For the six years before Alejandro came to the nuns, he had been locked in a closet and deprived of any stimulus while inhabitants of the house left each day for work. The nuns knew the boy could not be miraculously restored and spun from an imprisoning orbit into a new and enriched one, especially when the means to help him were limited. He was, after all, just one of forty boys with similar stories of poverty and neglect. I mention this because my knowledge of the Andean world, limited as it was and still is, meant that I could not separate myself from 'lived experience' to imaginatively enter Ann's fanciful novel. How could I believe that among her fictional terrorists, three were savants: a genius of language (who initially spoke only Quechua), a master of chess (though he had never played before), and a musical wunderkind with a voice to rival that of the famous opera diva, Roxanne.

The dark forms of naked trees throw another image my way—of a string quartet of Jewish prisoners playing Bach outside a crematorium in Nazi Germany. In the land of Goethe, Schiller, and Beethoven, did geniuses like these three giants of Western cultural arts, spin the bitter, defeated Germans into an orbit that kept them beyond the gravitational force of a heinous demigod and his perverted Nazi ideology?

In her novel of a real event, Ann Patchett's conceit is the idea that people would be kind and finely tuned if they were sequestered and given daily infusions of opera. This assumes, however, that indigenous, anti-imperialist revolutionaries would be enamored of opera, an art form of Western culture. In Jacques Barzun's masterful *From Dawn to Decadence (1500 to the Present)*, this historian writes of the need for the ear to become accustomed to the musical nuances of 17th century music like opera. "Another proof," he writes, "that music is not a homogeneous substance for all good ears to enjoy as soon as heard." The novelist Ann Patchett would have it otherwise. In *Bel Canto*, the government's military forces outside the residence also relish the diva's voice. But in real life, the Fujimori government blasted patriotic songs from a loudspeaker day and night to hide the noise of their tunnel construction into the Japanese ambassador's residence.

I wonder if Ann Patchett had qualms about borrowing a real event for her novel. Did she question whether she knew enough about Andean culture to understand the minds of those who choose revolution and terror as their means to effect change? *Bel Canto* is not the magic realism famous in South America, the most noteworthy author being the late Gabriel Garcia Marquez. But *Bel Canto* could be classified as fantasy-faction. In saying this, I reveal a bias; that I find something unsavory about literary fiction that offers the wish fulfillment of a romantic Hollywood movie.

After re-reading *Bel Canto*, I read reviews on the internet from readers, most of whom were unaware of the actual event in South America. Many lamented that the love story did not have a happy ending for the terrorists, despite Patchett's early foreshadowing of their inevitable deaths. In the novel's epilogue, however, she gives her readers a happy ending. In the idyllic setting of Puccini's birthplace, a surprise marriage takes place between the diva Roxanne and the translation savant, Gen. Otherwise, except for this one foreign setting, the reader never leaves the residence in *Bel Canto's* mythical, unnamed country and city; and this allows Patchett to do whatever she desires inside her limited, invented territory.

One thing about the setting is real. Ann Patchett obviously read about Lima's *garúa* and uses it. Beginning in chapter four, the narrator tells us: "The voices (soldiers in the street) couldn't always penetrate the fog. The *garúa* maintained a dull, irregular presence from April through November, and Father Arguedas said to take heart since October was very nearly over and then the sun

149

would return." At least the real hostages like Carlos did not have to contend with the *garúa* in December of 1996. Which is why Carlos so clearly saw the bird in the ambassador's garden the day of his release. And this image spun him to the day on his terrace during summer, at the time of the strange fog that shrouds Lima and pushes its suicide rates. It was the *garúa* that caused the dove's imprint to remain on Carlos's window, and why he wrote on it, *tiempo detenido*.

In again mentioning Carlos, I must acknowledge that he and Ann share a belief that our lives should be crowded with beauty. And Ann Patchett's beautiful prose resembles the clear, smooth, white porcelain that Carlos would like to make if he had more time. I think it is this talented writer's polished prose that seduces readers and critics, and why *Bel Canto* won both the Orange prize and the Pen/Faulkner.

The point of view in the novel is omniscient, which means the narrator is the goddess and creator of every character, and the sole proprietor of their thoughts and actions. By her own admission in a television interview and in articles, Patchett has stated that she cannot conceive of evil characters. She renames the real life MRTA, *La Familia de Martin Suarez*, a name that makes them sound harmless, despite their weapons and the early attack on the unnamed country's Vice-President, who bears his wounds with honor. *La Familia* is basically a loveable group. They enjoy television and chess, and they adore the famous opera star, Roxanne, whose singing reaches into their hearts. The residence is a glorified hotel (no mention of toilets and the fact that water to the actual residence was cut off). The French ambassador, a wife and wine-loving man, takes over the cooking. The Vice-President whose origins are humble is only too happy to play the role of cross-dressing servant, the *ama de casa*, keeping the residence

clean and tidy. And in another servile role, the Japanese Gen Wata-
nabe is ever available to translate the multiple languages spoken
among the hostages and terrorists, which solves a big problem for
the writer. Lastly, the kind priest, Father Arguedas, has Roxanne's
requested sheet music delivered to the residence like pizza.

To my eye and ear, the intrusive, authorial, omniscient narrator of *Bel Canto* has the feel of parody. I cannot accept that Ann
Patchett is so naïve as to believe the fantasy she creates. Did she
explore the rough landscape of Quechua-speaking Indians in Peru
where both the *Sendero* and the Peruvian military recruited soldiers? The poor and marginalized in Andean countries must serve
their mandatory military service, while those of economic means
are able to bribe and obtain exemptions. I recall the soldiers who
cared for horses at the army base where my daughter rode in Caracas. Many had never seen a toilet before they arrived in the
capital. Only if I had no knowledge of the politics and history of
the Andean region of South America, could I enter *Bel Canto's*
territory and live with its imaginary characters. Perhaps this is my
limitation, my *tiempo detenido*; that increasingly I cannot separate myself from lived experience to enter the lives of imaginary
characters in so many of the commercial, internet-driven novels
being published and promoted today.

Yet if I *were* able to enter Patchett's created territory, what
would I discover from wandering around in it? I would encounter
the fanciful notion that the world can be saved from bloody conflict through the beauty of art, that humans are capable of understanding each other beyond the languages spoken or not spoken;
that despite our diverse cultures and the preponderance of poverty
and the lack of education in countries like Peru, we can rise to a
heaven on earth and be united in love. I can only say that I would
have to be an innocent with little experience in the world to be

seduced by the fantasy of *Bel Canto*.

The humble clay of the potter, the unaltered image of the photographer, the polished prose of an award-winning writer: three artists in arrested time. Yet from within my *tiempo detenido*, I begin to feel a vein of repair. And with this feeling comes a renewed creative conviction to never knowingly give false maps to readers. I must describe the sea of life as it is—fathomless, vast, perilous, and joyful—and dedicate myself to prose that might serve as a blood transfusion, not a sugared, weak-tea version of life.

As an aging woman, I often wander the Chesapeake Bay where water meets land—observing crabs on the shoreline and feeling gratitude for the circle game in which we look behind from where we came. And while walking along, carried by wind and water, I reaffirm my belief in continuing to write—moving my pen freely and fearlessly, daring to tell hard, exacting truths.

Three Artists in Arrested Time
NLAPW Vinnie Ream Competition, 2019
Overall 2nd Place of three genres

CPSIA information can be obtained
at www.ICGtesting.com
Printed in the USA
BVHW062310081021
618238BV00002B/9

9 781734 160246